In Search of a Good Fit

The Student's Guide to Career Planning & College Preparation

By

John Schwaiger

In Search of a Good Fit
By
John Schwaiger

Printed in the United States of America

ISBN 978-0-578-11552-8

Dedicated to

Dr. Connie B. Schwaiger…

...My Shotize (Treasured Sweetheart), for your tremendous love, encouragement and support for the past 35 years. I am eternally grateful to God for giving me you as my wife and best friend.

The What, Why and How

Forward

What is your personality type? Do you know what your passion is? What makes you unique? What are natural abilities you are good at and how will all these things build or affect your career selection and preparation?

It was the first time in my life I was challenged to seriously consider the answers to these questions. Dr. John Schwaiger, the president of Careerformation, Inc., was not only asking tough questions but, wisely, helping us understands who we are and discover the career options that would best fit our personality, abilities and interests. It made perfect sense to look at your career and college as a **glove** that should perfectly fit your hand – your unique combination of personality, passion, abilities and interests. Our educational and workplace environment should challenge us to grow, to do things with passion and enthusiasm, to do our best and be our best.

I have been working with high school and university students for the past 15 years, I have made a passion for helping students, and young professionals find the career that will maximize their potential and satisfy them. Sadly, many young people still choose a direction in life based on their perception on what is trendy, brings a lot of money and an unrealistic perspective of the job market.

What will make you stand out among thousands of students just like you, at exactly the same stage in life? It is not an easy question when you start pondering on it and certainly, the answer is not at all easy. There are thousands of high school students like you, with big dreams, energy packed enthusiastic and wanting to prepare for and have a the right career that will be satisfying and successful. Employers seek experience, proven success, passion, organizational and leadership skills. Your college degree and educational background are only the minimum necessary and there are still thousands competing with you, who you know, may get you the job but it, certainly, will not help you keep it. There are a thousand students like you who start preparing for and pursuing a career that is not the right fit for them; there are only a few students who do.

So, what will make you stand out? What will make you successful? What will make you be different from all those who start with big dreams but end up with unrealistic dreams, in unsatisfying careers, frustrated, defeated, too scared to try again?

I have no doubt that this guide will help you start a wonderful but challenging process of self-discovery and help you, as it helped me and many other students to begin discovering and preparing for a realistic and rewarding career that would be the right fit for you.

Elvis Filote

Cru Representative

Table of
Contents

Why, Definition, Stages and Prerequisites

Essential Starting Point

Discovering Who I am and My Potential

Stage I – Identification

Discovering My Career Interests and Options

Stage II - Exploration

Preparing for College and My Career

Stage III – Preparation

Where Am I heading?

Stage IV – Goals

Marketing Myself

Stage V - Campaign

Reviewing Trends and Their Potential Impact

Stage VI – Trends

How Am I Doing?

Stage VII- Assessment

In Search of a Good Fit

Introduction

One cold afternoon, I went to the mall to get a new pair of gloves. As I walked into the glove department in the store, I noticed a gentleman looking for a pair of work gloves and a lady looking for a pair of dress gloves. I watched as the gentleman tried on a pair that seemed quite tight and he had a difficult time putting them on. As he tried the tight gloves, I noticed the expression on his face. It was one frustration after another. When he finally got them on, he looked uncomfortable and could not freely move his hand. He immediately tried to take them off and showed an expression of additional frustration. Then I watch a lady looking for a pair dress glove. She found and tried on a pair that was quite large. Her reaction was that these gloves were too bulky and cumbersome. Then she tried a second pair, which was too small, uncomfortable and restricted her hand's movement. Then I went to look for a pair of gloves myself. One pair was blue and seemed a little tight and uncomfortable. Then I tried a black pair that, to my surprise, fit quite well. I got them on easily and was able to move my hand freely without exerting any effort. I thought to myself, "what a good fit," and purchase them! That afternoon the gentleman, lady and I had one goal in mind-to buy a pair of gloves that would fit our hands and function in the manner for which they were intended.

The above hand-glove illustration depicts the main theme of this guide. The **hand** represents your personality and its unique characteristics, and the **glove** is your career and college options. The objectives of this guide are to empower you to begin reviewing and answering the following key questions:

What is my personality type and its potential influence and impact on my career options? - **Hand**

What are my realistic and rewarding career options? - **Glove**

How do I effectively plan and prepare for a satisfying and successful career that, utilizes my personality and its unique characteristics? – **The Good Fit**

The ultimate goal of this guide is to equip and empower you in discovering the career you can love and the right college to prepare you for your selected career!

John Schwaiger
Goshen, Massachusetts, USA

Why, Definition, Stages and Prerequisites

Essential Starting Point

A student was walking across campus to chapel in his first year in college, God quietly approached him and said, "I have a wonderful mission for you to accomplish!" The student immediately replied, "Who me?" I am no one special, have no special gifts. You have the wrong person." God's response to the student was, "Yes. I do have the right person. You just do not know it yet. You will in time." Years later, this student who graduated from college and even completed an MBA was flying home from a European business trip. As he was flying over the Atlantic Ocean, God again quietly talked to the individual who felt that God had the wrong person. He asked, "Well, what do you think about my saying 'I have something wonderful for you to accomplish?" His response was, "Lord, I am sorry for doubting you. Since you last talked to me, I have discovered that you have:

Created me with a unique personality that makes me, one of a kind and unique.

Enabled me to find the right fit between my **hand** (personality and its unique characteristics) and **gloves** (college and career) and

Equipped me with the **resources** (passion, abilities and interests) to faithfully complete the **responsibilities** (career/ministry) you have entrusted to me."

That is what the career planning and college preparation process are all about! It equips and enables you to begin discovering and developing your God-Given life's purpose and potential. What makes this process challenging are the major changes taking place in today's educational, economic and technical landscape. These changes impacting today's employment opportunities and are influencing the development of tomorrow's careers. Therefore, preparing for the right career requires careful planning and preparation. It will allow you to find the best fit between **hand - your unique personality** and **glove - your career** and effectively prepare for the changing and competitive marketplace. However, before you can begin your career planning and college preparation it will be essential for you to review Creator, Creation & Creation's Managers. The objectives of reviewing Creator, Creation, and Creation's Managers are to **gain** a proper understanding of who is the Creator and your relationship to Him; **appreciate** the wonder and beauty of His creation handiwork, and **discover** the purpose for which you were created.

Creator: Let me ask you a question: "When you think of who the Creator is, what comes to your mind?" Let us look at the Scripture's descriptions of your Creator:

In the beginning, God created the heavens and the earth. ***Genesis 1:1a***

Who has understood the mind of the Lord, or instructed him as his counselor?

Whom did the Lord consult to enlighten him, and who taught him the right way? Who was it that taught him knowledge or showed him the path of understanding? ***Isaiah 40:13-14***

> *Through him, all things were made; without him nothing was made that has been made.* **John 1:3a**

Creation: As you took a brief look at God, you discovered that he is all knowing (omniscient), all present (omnipresent) and all powerful (omnipotent). Now you will find out what the Scriptures have to say about his magnificent creation:

> *For by him all things were created: things in the heavens and on earth, visible and invisible, whether thrones or powers or rulers or authorities; all things were created by him and for him. He is before all things, and in him, all things hold together.* **Colossians 1:16-17**

> *When I consider your heavens, the work of your fingers, the moon and the stars, which you have set in place.* **Psalms 8:3**

> *The heavens declare the glory of God; the skies proclaim the work of his hands. Day after day they pour forth speech; night after night they display knowledge.* **Psalm 19:1-2**

Creation's Managers: Can you believe that an omniscient, omnipresent and omnipotent God, who has created heaven and earth, has created you as His creation's manager? Creation's managers are:

> ***Created in God's Image & Character**: Then God said, "Let us make man in our image in our likeness, and let them rule over the fish of the sea and the birds of the air, over the livestock, over all the earth, and over all the creatures that move along the ground."* **Genesis 1:26**

> ***Co-Managers of God's Creation:** You have made him a little lower than the heavenly beings, crowned him with glory and honor and charged to rule over the works of his hands; you put everything under his feet.* **Psalm 8:5-6**

> ***Fearfully, Wonderfully & Purposefully Created:** For you created my inmost being, you knit me together in my mother's womb. I praise you because I am fearfully and wonderfully made; your works are wonderful, I know that full well. My frame was not hidden from you, when I was made in the secret place. When I was woven together in the depths of the earth, your eyes saw my unformed body. All the days ordained for me were written in your book before one of them came to be. How precious to me are your thoughts, O God! How vast is the sum of them! Were I to count them, they would outnumber the grains of sand.* **Psalm 139:13-18a**

God's Co-Workers Hall of Fame: Now look at several examples of God's co-workers and the contributions they made:

Adam named the animals so that we would know what to call them.

Noah built an ark so that we could be here today.

Moses delivered the Ten Commandments so we would know how to behave.

Mary gave birth to Jesus Christ, the Son of God, so that we could be redeemed.

A little boy offered his lunch to Jesus to feed five thousand people, revealing how God meets needs in unusual ways.

Esther risked her life to preserve her people, revealing how God protects his own.

The widow fed Elijah with only a handful of flour and a little oil, revealing how God provides for those who put their trust in Him.

What thoughts ran through your mind as you learn about God's co-workers and their contributions in the examples given?

Was it "Wow!" Or "Not me!" If your response was, like the student, "Not me," God says, "Yes, You!" God made you unique so that you can achieve something that no one else can. *For we are God's workmanship, created in Christ Jesus to do good works, which God prepared in advance for us to do,* ***Ephesians 2:10.*** Therefore, as his co-workers, you will need to begin finding answers to the following questions:

1. Why did God create me?

2. What does God want to accomplish through my life?

3. What contributions can I make to His creation?

Finding answers to these and other questions is the goal of the career planning process. This can be an exciting, life-changing learning opportunity for you. However, before you can proceed with career planning, it is essential for you to identify what your priorities are.

Priorities are what are most influential in your life. It is God's desire for you, as his co-worker, to establish the following three priorities:

1. **Loving** Him wholeheartedly and your fellow man unconditionally. **Mark 12:30-31**

2. **Seeking** God's kingdom and righteousness. **Matthew 6:33**

3. **Investing** your life into furthering His eternal kingdom on earth. **Matthew 6:19-20**

Now you are ready to begin discovering what God has in store for you, what career and college road he wants you to travel. You may be asking when is the ideal time to start developing your career planning program. College admission counselors strongly recommended that high school students begin this essential process in their freshmen year in high school. In doing so, you and your parents will have the time necessary to begin career planning and preparing for college without feeling rushed, which can then become a less stressful and rewarding experience.

Definition: Career Planning is a systematic, continual, and realistic process of exploring, investigating, evaluating, and selecting a rewarding career that honors God and utilizes your God-given abilities. This process enables you to:

1. **Discover** the right career path for you to travel

2. **Know** that you are heading in the right direction with **confidence- head** and **conviction** – **heart**

3. **Achieve** your God-given purpose and potential

Stages: The career planning & college preparation process incorporates the following seven stages:

1. **Identification** - Who am I? What is my personality type, passion, abilities, skills, values, interests, etc.?

2. **Evaluation** - What is the best fit between my **hand** – personality and **gloves** careers and colleges?

3. **Preparation** - How should I effectively prepare for my selected career and the marketplace?

4. **Goals** -What are my career and college goals, if any?

5. **Campaign** - What is the best strategy for obtaining a rewarding position in my selected field after graduation?

6. **Trends** -What is the future predicted in my selected career and in the marketplace.

7. **Assessment** – How am I doing in college or vocational school and in my career?

Promises: Carefully and prayerfully, review the following advice and promises God gives you as you start planning for your future:

1. *Trust in the Lord with all your heart, and lean not on your own understanding; in all your ways acknowledge Him and He will make your paths straight.* ***Proverbs 3:5-6***

2. *Commit to the Lord whatever you do, and your plans will succeed.* ***Proverbs 16:3***

3. *In his heart, a man plans his course, but the Lord determines his steps.* ***Proverbs 16:9***

As you start planning for your career and college, carefully answer the following prerequisite questions:

1. In your own words, what does God say about planning and preparing for your future career and college in Proverbs 3:5-6?

2. Explain in your own words why Proverbs 15:22 strongly encourages you to seek guidance in planning and preparing for your future.

3. Explain in your own words what God has to say about you in, Ephesians 2:10?

4. What three principles is God communicating to you in James 4:13-15 as you plan for your future?

a.____

____

____

b.____

____

____

c.____

____

____

5. What career or careers are you interested in preparing for in college, if you know?

a. ______________________________

____

____

b. ______________________________

____

____

c. ______________________________

____

____

6. What are your three career planning objectives?

a. ______________________________

____

____

b. ______________________________

____

____

c. ______________________________

____

____

7. List three potential challenges you may face in your career and college planning and preparation.

a.____

____

____

b.____

____

____

c.____

____

____

Discovering Who I am and My Potential

Stage I - Identification

"I personally believe that each of us was put here for a purpose -- to build not to destroy. If I can make people smile, then I have served my purpose for God." ***Red Skelton***

There are two questions I like to ask people. Two questions that may appear to be simple to answer; but actually have caused students and adults struggle to answer. They are **"Who are you?"** and **"What do you hope to accomplish in life?"** These two questions are so closely linked together that one cannot be answered without the other. The first stage of the career planning process is where you begin finding answers to these questions. **Internal Audit** is the first part of the identification stage. However, before beginning the internal audit, it is essential to recollect that you are created in God's image and character Genesis 1:26 that provide you with the foundation of self-worth. Secondly, you are **fearfully** and **wonderfully made Psalm 139:14** that **motivate** you to accept and appreciate others and yourself. Finally, you are a **masterpiece** of God's creation **Ephesians 2:10a** that encourages you to treat others and yourself with dignity and respect.

Sound Auditing Process

Sound Auditing Process is an examination of one's assets and liabilities. Organizations regularly conducts internal and external audits to **identify** their assets and liabilities in order to **maintain** their peak performance and **achieve** the organizations' goals. Similarly, to select, prepare for and manage a satisfying, successful, and God-honoring career requires that you conduct a sound internal and external audit, which is an essential part of the Sound Auditing Process. By completing this audit, you will begin finding answers to the following questions.

1. What makes me unique and special?

2. What is my passion - why do I do what I do?

3. What accomplishments am I proud of?

4. What do I enjoy and not enjoy doing?

5. What are my natural abilities, interests, and values?

6. What type of environment am I comfortable in?

7. How do I relate to the people around me?

The Sound Auditing Process includes the following: **Identifying** your **personality type** – what makes you unique, **Motivational pattern/passion** – why you do what you do, **Achievements/abilities** – what you enjoy doing and do well, and **career options** - that interest and fit you.

Personality Type: Your personality and its unique characteristics make you one of a kind out of 7+ Billion people living in this world today! It is essential to define personality and what personality type is before conducting a personality type audit. **Personality** is the total of the physical, mental, emotional, social and behavioral characteristics of a person. **Personality type** is the general classifications of a personality, its functions and operating styles. It is essential to go through the following steps in order to begin identifying and understanding your personality type and its unique characteristics.

1. **Complete** a personality indicator such as MBTI® and/or DISC. ® The Personality Type Indicator MBTI with 93 questions will **identify** your potential personality type out of a category of 16 personality types, **describe** your preferred functions and operating styles and **measure** the clarity of your personality type and its functions and operating styles.

2. **Attend** an Introduction to Personality Type class or schedule a counseling session with a qualified counselor who can accurately explain your results and answer questions. This is essential to avoid any misunderstanding or wrong interpretation of your results that can be seriously misleading and harmful. The personality indicator is a powerful and helpful tool if properly understood. It will enable you to gain insights and understanding your personality type and its unique characteristics.

3. **Read** reference materials to learn more and understand further different personality types, their four preferred functions, and two opposite operating styles. Recommended reference materials such as:

   Introduction to Types, by Roger R. Pearson & Sarah C Albritton

   I'M *Not Crazy, I'M Just Not Like You – Secrets to How We Can be So Alike, When We're So Different,* by Isabel B. Myers

As you review your personality indicator results, it is essential to remember:

1. Only you can confirm what you think your personality type is and the personality indicator reports what may be your potential personality type.

2. Personality type reports that not clearly defined may be a result of one's personality type still developing.

3. All personalities that God has created are equally good, important, valuable, and should be accepted, appreciated and respected.

Completing a personality type indicator is just one of the essential tools in the career planning and the college preparation process. As stated earlier, it provides insights into your God-given personality and its unique characteristic, which in turn enables you to accurately identify, evaluate and select the career and college that would best fit you. The next step in the Sound Auditing Process is to begin identifying and reading your motivational pattern/passion -"Why you do what you do?" which is the aim of the next audit.

Central Motivational Pattern: The motivation pattern is evidence that God has designed us not as haphazard collections of possibilities, but people with highly, detailed gifts that differ from one individual to another. Those gifts emerge from the depths of our motivates and determine our place in the scheme of things. As each animal and organism functions in a particular place in God's creation, so we too, are designed for a particular role in the human community and in the world. [1]

The central motivational pattern is a common thread tying together all the things you do well: a single overriding and unifying reason for why you do what you do. It plays a dominant role in your life because it is permanent, consistent, and controls your behavior. [2]

In *Finding a Job You Can Love*, Mattson and Miller have identified the following eighteen central motivational patterns:

Acquire/possess money, material things and status.

Be in charge/command of others, things and organizations.

Combat/prevail over current status quo, adversaries, evil and opposing philosophies.

Develop/build something new physical and technical.

Excel/be the best compared to others and conventional standards.

Exploit/achieve potential situations, market, things and people.

Gain response/influence behavior from people through people and react to my potential influence in their thinking, attitudes and actions.

Gain recognition/attention from people, groups and public officials, being famous and in the spotlight.

Improve/make better self, others, work and organizations.

Make the team/grade by gaining access to groups and organizations.

Meet needs/fulfill expectations by fulfilling customers, bosses expressed wants and needs.

Make work/make more effective repair things, improve and update operations, and redesign, what was poorly made.

Master/perfect subject, skills, equipment and things.

Organize/operate efficiently established team, business and product

Overcome/persevere over obstacles, handicaps, unknown and odds.

Pioneer/explore new organizations, technology, cultures and ideas.

Serve/help people, organizations and causes.

Shape/Influence people's thinking, attitudes and actions.[3]

"How can I know and confirm what my motivational pattern/passion is?" is a question you may be asking. You can find the answer to this question by completing the following three-step process:

First, review the definition of what the motivational pattern is. "**The motivational pattern** is a common thread tying together all the things you do well: a single overriding and unifying reason for why you do what you do. It plays a dominant role in your life because it is permanent, consistent, and controls your behavior."[4]

Second, review carefully the list of 18 Central Motivational Patterns in this guide and select the ones you think may be yours.

Finally, complete the Achievement/Abilities Audit to identify and confirm what your motivational pattern may be.

Achievements/Abilities Audit enables you to identify those enjoyable accomplishments that you had direct responsibility in planning, developing and successfully completing. By completing this audit you will gain new insights and answers to the "What you are naturally gifted in doing question?" In *The Great Niche Hunt,* David Frahm, gives following benefits in carefully completing an achievement/abilities audit:

Your past contains road signs that point toward your future. Your most enjoyable accomplishments reveal the fabric of your future. Once you've discovered in them the threads of your functional design, you can make knowledgeable, perceptive career choices that allow you to reflect who you really are. [3]

A careful and comprehensive completion of this audit enables you to begin identifying and seeing what your God-given abilities are; subject matters you enjoy working with and talking about; circumstance you are comfortable with; and how you connect with others. This audit also offers insights into what your motivational pattern/passion may be. If properly completed, it can become a rich and rewarding experience, which objectively answers: "Who you are and what you can do naturally well questions?" It will provide you with critical information needed, when you begin to identify, explore, evaluate, and select a satisfying, and successful career that best fits you. To begin your achievements/abilities audit review and complete the following seven steps.

1. **Review** and **identify** your past enjoyable achievements. Experiences that you had direct responsibility for planning, preparing and completing.

2. **Select** and **write** down in detail, (what you did, how you did it and when), seven of your most enjoyable achievements in the Achievement List – My 7 Achievements Worksheet in this guide.

3. **Review** the Action Verbs List in this guide

4. **Identify** those verbs used in your achievements and **list** them in the Verbs List Section of **Achievements List - My 7 Achievements Worksheet**.

5. **Identify** and **Circle** the five to eight most frequently used action verbs from your Verbs List.

6. **Review** the following eighteen ability groupings, identified by Mattson and Miller:

   - **An *investigative* ability**: interview, experiment
   - **A *learning* ability**: observe, research, study, practice
   - **A *visualizing* ability**: conceptualize, picture, dream
   - **An *evaluating* ability**: analyze, assess, select
   - **A *formulating* ability**: theorize, define
   - **A *planning* ability**: design, layout, schedule, strategize
   - **A *creating* ability**: invent, improvise, innovate, paint
   - **An *organizing* ability**: collect, synthesize, systematize
   - **A *developing* ability**: improve, tinker, modify

- A ***constructing* ability**: build, assemble, put together
- **An *operating* ability**: manage, administer, manipulate
- **An *implementing* ability**: do physically, execute
- A ***counseling* ability**: coach, advise
- A ***supervising* ability**: lead, coordinate, direct
- A ***performing* ability**: act, demonstrate, dance, speak
- A ***teaching* ability**: train, instruct, explain, demonstrate
- A ***writing* ability**: edit, compose, advertise
- **An *influencing* ability**: convince, advocate, motivate and sell. [4]

7. **Group** those five to eight verbs most frequently used in your achievements into the ability groupings that best fits their description as illustrated below:

   A teaching ability: Instructed students in the proper used on credit cards; explained the pitfalls of misuse of credit cards; and illustrated examples of individuals who have misused their credit cards.

   An influencing ability: Motivated students begin discovering their God-given abilities by completing an achievement/abilities audit; **persuaded** students about the need to think through their reasons for going or not going to college; and **recommended** students carefully consider establishing realistic and reachable career goals.

   An organizing ability: Scheduled and **conducted** monthly yearbook staff meetings; **delegated** yearbook staff assignments, and **coordinated** photographs needed to convey the yearbook's theme

Now that you have started the first part of the identification process: (discovering your personality type, enjoyable achievements, natural abilities, and motivational pattern), it is time to move to the second part of the designation procedure, which is identifying potential career options that best suits you.

Aptitude Test & Interest Inventory

This fourth and final part of the Sound Auditing Process involves **completing** a General Aptitude Test Battery and/or Vocational Interest Inventory.

The General Aptitude Test Battery is also known as the **GATB**, it is a series of **twelve** (**eight** – paper and pencil, and **four** – computerized) tests. These tests assess your aptitude in nine different areas and evaluate your chances to be successful in specific careers or training programs.

The Vocational Interest Inventory is an inventory of your career interests not abilities. It enables you to **identify** your consistency of vocational likes and dislikes and occupational orientation in six occupational themes. It allows you to **measure** the degree of similarity of your responses as compared to the individual responses, interests and characteristics of your gender currently working in those occupations. It **describes** the different ways you approach people, learning, leading, making decisions and working on teams.

It is essential to note that a vocational interest inventory **is an inventory, not a test**. There are no right or wrong answers or passing or failing grade attached to it.

The Personality Type Indicator, General Aptitude Test Battery, and Vocational Inventory results will **confirm** what you already know about your personality and vocational interests. They will **provide** new insights into yourself and **give** you confidence to pursue a career that you are considering. They also will offer alternative career options that you may not have considered.

A word of caution: It is not recommended to make a sound career decision based on just one of these assessment tools! Making well thought-out and wise career choices are based on completing all four audits in the Sound Auditing Process.

Hand - Glove Principle

Once you have identified your personality type, past enjoyable achievements, motivational pattern, passion and career options, then you can begin the hand-glove process. It is the process of finding the right fit between your **hand** – your unique personality and **glove** – career options. Again, it is essential to remember that completing the Sound Auditing Process can be a very rich and rewarding experience when properly completed. This will provide you with a solid foundation from which you can begin the next step.

1. **Discover** new insights about yourself

2. **Identify** and **evaluate** career options that best fit you and

3. **Develop** and **manage** a satisfying, successful and God-honoring career.

A word of caution is in order. Conducting a Sound Auditing Process is not a once in a lifetime exercise, but a continual process throughout your life!

Action Verb

List

Accelerated
Accumulated
Acted
Adapted
Addressed
Adjusted
Advised
Altered
Analyzed
Anticipated
Applied
Appraised
Arbitrated
Arranged
Ascertained
Assembled
Assessed
Assisted
Attained
Audited
Budgeted
Built
Calculated
Changed
Charted
Clarified
Classified
Cleaned
Cleared
Coached
Collected
Communicated
Compared
Completed
Complied
Composed
Computed
Conceptualized
Conducted
Conserved
Consolidated
Constructed
Consulted
Contacted
Controlled
Converted
Coordinated
Correlated

Counseled
Created
Decided
Defined
Delegated
Delivered
Demonstrated
Derived
Designed
Detailed
Detected
Determined
Devised
Diagnosed
Directed
Dispensed
Displayed
Disproved
Dissected
Distributed
Earned
Edited
Eliminated
Encouraged
Enforced
Engaged
Engineered
Established
Estimated
Evaluated
Examined
Exhibited
Expanded
Expedited
Experimented
Explained
Expressed
Extracted
Filed
Financed
Followed
Forecasted
Formulated
Founded
Gathered
Generated
Guided
Handled

Headed
Illustrated
Implemented
Improved
Improvised
Increased
Influenced
Informed
Initiated
Innovated
Inspected
Inspired
Installed
Instituted
Instructed
Integrated
Interpreted
Interviewed
Introduced
Invented
Inventoried
Investigated
Judged
Justified
Launched
Learned
Lectured
Led
Lifted
Listened
Made
Maintained
Managed
Marketed
Mediated
Memorized
Met
Modeled
Monitored
Motivated
Moved
Navigated
Negotiated
Notified
Observed
Obtained
Offered
Opened

Operated
Ordered
Originated
Packed
Painted
Participated
Perceived
Performed
Persuaded
Photographed
Piloted
Pinpointed
Pioneered
Planned
Played
Predicted
Prepared
Prescribed
Presented
Printed
Processed
Produced
Programmed
Projected
Promoted
Proposed
Protected
Proved
Provided
Publicized
Purchased
Questioned
Raised
Reasoned
Received
Recommended
Reconciled
Recorded
Recruited
Reduced
Regulated
Rehabilitated
Reinforced
Rendered
Reorganized
Repaired
Reported
Represented

Researched
Responded
Restored
Retrieved
Reviewed
Scheduled
Screened
Selected
Sensed
Separated
Served
Set
Shaped
Shared
Shipped
Simplified
Sketched
Solved
Sorted
Spoke
Stimulated
Studied
Submitted
Succeeded
Summarized
Supervised
Supplied
Supported
Surveyed
Symbolized
Synthesized
Systematized
Tailored
Tended
Tested
Trained
Transcribed
Transferred
Translated
Transmitted
Traveled
Tutored
Unified
United
Utilized
Verified
Weighed
Wrote

My List of 7 Achievements

Worksheet

Achievement Number 1: Ambassador Yearbook. **Date: 2011**

During my junior year in college: I was chief editor of the yearbook. As chief editor, I was responsible for **selecting** the yearbook's theme, basic layout, materials, and publisher. I **selected** and **managed a** staff of 28 personnel. I **scheduled** and **conducted** monthly staff meetings, resulting in **improved** staff relations and performance. I **delegated** staff assignments and assisted when needed. I **coordinated** photographs needed to convey on the yearbook's theme. All deadlines were met ahead of schedule resulting in early delivery.

Verb List

Selecting
Managed
Scheduled
Conducted
Improved
Delegated
Coordinated

Achievement # 1________________________________**Date**__________

Verbs List

Achievement # 2________________________________**Date**__________

Verbs List

Achievement # 3____________________ **Date**________ **Verbs List**

Achievement # 4____________________ **Date**________ **Verbs List**

Achievement # 5____________________ **Date**________ **Verbs List**

Achievement # 6______________________________**Date**__________ **Verbs List**

Achievement # 7______________________________**Date**__________ **Verbs List**

What I Learned from Completing My Audits

Worksheet

My Seven Achievements are:

1. ______________________________
2. ______________________________
3. ______________________________
4. ______________________________
5. ______________________________
6. ______________________________
7. ______________________________

My Central Motivational Pattern: ______________________________

My identified natural abilities are:

1. ______________________________
2. ______________________________
3. ______________________________
4. ______________________________
5. ______________________________
6. ______________________________
7. ______________________________

My identified natural abilities (action verbs) fall into the following groupings:

- **An *investigative* ability**: ____________ ____________ ____________
- **A *learning* ability**: ____________ ____________ ____________

- **A *visualizing* ability:** __________ __________ __________
- **An *evaluating* ability:** __________ __________ __________
- **A *formulating* ability:** __________ __________ __________
- **A *planning* ability:** __________ __________ __________
- **A *creating* ability:** __________ __________ __________
- **An *organizing* ability:** __________ __________ __________
- **A *developing* ability:** __________ __________ __________
- **A *constructing* ability:** __________ __________ __________
- **An *operating* ability:** __________ __________ __________
- **An *implementing* ability:** __________ __________ __________
- **A *counseling* ability:** __________ __________ __________
- **A *supervising* ability:** __________ __________ __________
- **A *performing* ability:** __________ __________ __________
- **A *teaching* ability:** __________ __________ __________
- **A *writing* ability:** __________ __________ __________
- **An *influencing* ability:** __________ __________ __________

Subject matters I enjoy talking about and dealing with are:

1. ____
2. ____
3. ____

Circumstances I am comfortable in are: ____________________________

____

I interact with people in following manner: ______________________________

____

____

My confirmed personality type is: ____________________ **or** ______________________

My occupational themes are:___________________________ - _____________________

My basic interests are:

1. ____
2. ____
3. ____

My three highest reported occupations are:

1. ____
2. ____
3. ____

I learned the following things about myself from completing my achievements: _________

____

____

____

I learned the following things about myself from completing the personality indicator: ____

____

____

____

I learned the following things about myself from completing: my interest inventory: ______

____

____

____

God has revealed the following three things about me and what makes me unique.

1. ____
2. ____
3. ____

Discovering My Career Interests and Options

Stage II -Exploration

The secret of concentration is the secret of self-discovery. You reach inside yourself to discover your personal resources, and what it takes to match them to the challenge. ***Arnold Palmer***

Now that you have begun working on your internal and external audit, you have begun gaining new insights into what makes you unique and why you do what you do. Again I want to remind you, that completing these audits is not a once-in-a-lifetime exercise but a lifelong process, because you continue to grow, change and learn new things about yourself and the world around you. Now, here is another question for consideration, **"What do you dream and hope of accomplishing in your life?"** When finishing the identification section of the seminar, I ask students this question. Over the years, I have received some unique answers.

> **Robert** who was a sophomore at Faith Academy, Manila, Philippines, dreamed about becoming president of the Philippines.
>
> **Susan,** who was a junior at Dakar Academy, Senegal, West Africa, dreamed about becoming a missionary doctor.
>
> **Matthew**, a senior at ICA in Ivory Coast, West Africa, shared his dreamed of designing cars.

Finding answers to the above mentioned questions is called the Exploration Step which is the second step in the Sound Career Selection Process. It is a process that incorporates: **Identifying**, **exploring**, **investigating** and **evaluating** your options, which is foundational to the sound career selection process.

The first step in the sound career selection process is where you begin thinking about and **identifying** what characteristics you are looking for in a career. In identifying your desired career characteristics, you need to begin asking and honestly answering the following questions.

1. What type of environment do I want to work in?

2. What abilities and activities do I want to use in my career?

3. What type of people do I want to work with?

The second cornerstone begins with **exploring** what your career options are. Let's begin the first step in exploring your options by answering the following questions.

1. Will the career I am considering utilizing my personality, passion, abilities and interests?

2. Will the career under consideration include those characteristics I have identified?

3. Will I have the ability, commitment and motivation to meet the educational and experience requirements to effectively prepare for the career choice?

To assist you in finding answers to the above questions requires you carefully and complete the following three essential steps:

1. **Select** three potential career options to explore.

2. **Go to** www.bls.gov/oco/

3. **Review** and **record** all related information pertinent to the career such as nature of the work, working conditions, employment, training, other qualifications, advancement, job outlook, earnings and other related occupations.

With the above steps initiated, you can begin investigating your potential selected career choices, by further **investigating** if they are realistic and reachable which is the third cornerstone in the sound career selection process. This is where you begin conducting informational interviews with professionals who are in careers you are considering. The three primary objectives of Informational interviews are:

1. **Gather** additional first hand insights and information on possible career options not available in the occupational outlook handbook or other printed materials

2. **Obtain** advice and recommendations regarding planning and preparing careers under consideration

3. **Evaluate** carefully all information and advice gathered gained from the interview

To achieve the above-mentioned objectives, it requires completing the following essential steps

1. **Identify** a list of individuals who are in the careers under consideration and who are willing to conduct informational interviews with you.

2. **Write** and **mail** career informational interview request letters to identify targeted individuals.

3. **Prepare, schedule** and **conduct** your informational interviews. It is essential that you be proactive in this threefold process, which will be covered later in this guide.

Now that, you have **identified** your desired career characteristics, **explored** your career choices and **investigated** your options, you are ready to **evaluate** your realistic career choices.

Realistic career choices that are a good fit between your **hand** - personality and **glove - career**. To complete the final step in the sound career selection process requires you to ask and answer the following questions:

1. What characteristics are included in my career options?

2. What are the personality, aptitude, abilities and skill requirements of the career?

3. What are the educational and experience requirements?

4. Will I have the ability, commitment and motivation to meet all of the career's requirements to effectively prepare for it?

The following is a good example of how successful the sound career selection process can be when properly implemented and completed.

> First she began **identifying** what characteristics she was looking for in a career. Then she set **exploring** what was involved in becoming a doctor and also looked into a possible nursing career. With the information gathered, she then started **investigating** what her realistic career options was by conducting informational interviews with several doctors and a nurse. Upon completing her information interviews, Hanna began **evaluating** what her realistic and reachable career options were and gained a clearer understanding of what the educational and experience requirements were for becoming a doctor and a nurse.

Finally these four crucial steps in the sound career selection process enabled Hanna to make a well thought-out and wise career choice. She decided with **confidence** – **head** and **conviction** – **heart** to become a nurse, rather than a doctor. Hanna first discovered it was a good and right fit between for her **hand** - personality and **glove** – career. She then also realized that she did not have the ability, motivation and commitment to complete twelve plus years of education to become a doctor. She also decided she did not want to go into deep debt to become a doctor.

Seven Key Things I Am Looking For in a Career!

Worksheet

1.____

2.____

3.____

4.____

5.____

6.____

7.____

Exploring My Career Options

Worksheet

1. **Select** three careers options.

2. **Download** or **copy** each career option from the *Occupational Outlook Handbook* located in your library or online at www.bls.gov.oco/

Career Selection # 1____

____

____

____

____

Career Selection # 2____

____

____

____

____

Career Selection # 3____

____

____

____

____

Investigating My Career Options

Worksheet

1. **Write** a career information request letter see sample letter in this guide.

2. **Review** objectives of the Informational Interview in this guide.

3. **Prepare** a list of interview questions; see the sample list of interview Career Questions in this guide.

4. **Think** of individuals who are in careers that you are considering and who would be willing to conduct an informational interview with you.

My List Contacts

Name of Contact #1:

Title:

Organization:

Address:

City: State: Zip:

Phone # E-mail:

Referred by:

Name of Contact #2:

Title:

Organization:

Address:

City: State: Zip:

Phone # E-mail:

Referred by:

Name of Contact #3: ____________________

Title: ____________________

Organization: ____________________

Address: ____________________

City: ____________ State: ____________ Zip ________

Phone # ____________ E-mail: ____________

Referred by: ____________________

My list of questions

1. ____________________

____

2. ____________________

____

3. ____________________

____

4. ____________________

____

5. ____________________

____

6. ____________________

____

7. ____________________

____

Requesting Information Interview

Sample Career Information Interview Letter

Jonathan D. Swartz
Pan Christian School
Apartado 19
Mexico
swartzjd@aol.com

April 19, 2013

Ms. Mary Brown
V.P. Marketing
First Bank of Virginia
1970 Chain Bridge Road
McLean, Virginia 22033

Dear Ms. Brown:

At the recommendation of Mr. Joseph Jones, my guidance counselor, I am sending you this letter.

I am a junior at Pan Christian School and am considering International Marketing as my major in college. I am currently gathering information on how to prepare for a career in international marketing. Mr. Jones recommended that I talk to individuals like you who are in this field.

I would greatly appreciate the opportunity to talk with you in person or over the phone about your career. I believe that an individual of your position, experience and knowledge could provide me with advice on how to prepare for this career.

I will call you shortly to schedule an appointment or to conduct a phone interview with you.

Thank you for your kind assistance in my career research project.

Sincerely,

Jonathan D. Swartz

Jonathan D. Swartz
High School Junior

Evaluating My Options

Worksheet

Please answer the following questions about careers you are considering.

Career Evaluation #1:____

1. What attracted you to this career?

____

____

2. Is there a good match between your personality type and this career choice?

____

____

3. Are you committed to meeting the educational and experience requirements for this career?

____

____

____

4. What are the personality characteristics requirements for this career? Check each personality attribute required for your chosen career.

Extravert_______ Introvert _______ or Both _______

Sensing ______ Intuition _______ or Both _______

Thinking ______ Feeling _______ or Both _______

Judging ______ Perceiving _____ or Both _______

Career Evaluation #2:____

1. What attracted you to this career?

____

____

2. Is there a good match between your personality type and this career choice?

____

____

3. Are you committed to meeting the educational and experience requirements for this career?

____

____

4. What are the personality characteristics requirements for this career? Check each personality attribute required for your chosen career.

Extravert_______ Introvert _______ or Both _______

Sensing ______ Intuition _______ or Both _______

Thinking ______ Feeling _______ or Both _______

Judging ______ Perceiving _____ or Both _______

Career Evaluation #3:____

1. What attracted you to this career?

____

____

2. Is there a good match between your personality type and this career choice?

____

____

3. Are you committed to meeting the educational and experience requirements for this career?

____

____

4. What are the personality characteristics requirements for this career? Check each personality attribute required for this career.

Extravert______ Introvert ______ or Both ______

Sensing ______ Intuition ______ or Both ______

Thinking ______ Feeling ______ or Both ______

Judging ______ Perceiving _____ or Both ______

Summary Evaluation

In completing your final career evaluation, read

For which of you, desires to build a tower, does not down first sit down and count the cost, whether he has enough to complete it? Otherwise, when he has laid the foundation and is not able to finish it. ***Luke 14:28-29***

Identify three key principles Luke wants you to apply in your final career selection.

1. ______________________________

____

____

____

2. ______________________________

____

____

____

3. ______________________________

____

____

____

Evaluating if The GAP Year is Right for Me

What Is It and Its Potential Benefits?

Today's high school students are searching answers to the following questions:

Gary, a senior, asked, "What is a GAP year?"
Alice, another senior, asked, "What criteria should I establish in planning for a GAP Year?"
Paul, a junior asked, "What are the benefits of taking a GAP year?"

Taking a GAP year has become an extremely attractive option for many high school students who want to:

Gain new exposures and experiences outside the traditional classroom environment
Address stress and burnout issues after a number of years in school
Pursue international learning and service opportunities.

Yearn for a break from studying in a formal academic environment
Earn money to help pay college expenses
Assess their educational and vocational goal and objectives
Renew their motivation and purpose for pursuing higher education

The Gap Year is defined as taking a year or two away from full time academic studies to pursue other interests and experiences. It is known as a **year abroad**, a **year out**, a **year off**, or a **deferred year**. Normally, it starts after high school graduation and before starting college. Lately, there has been an increase in 21-23 year olds taking a gap year after completing their degree.

The **objectives**, criteria and benefits of taking a gap year are:

Gain new experiences and exposures to other facets of life and cultures, providing perspective and guidance for a more meaningful and purposeful college experience.
Assess occupational and educational direction.
Provide opportunities for the development of maturity, independence and self-confidence through various paid and volunteer experiences.

Criteria to effect plan and prepare for a productive GAP year requires:

Giving legitimate and well-thought out reasons for taking a gap year
Assembling the GAP year's goal and objectives
Planning and preparing affecting every aspect of your GAP year

Yielding every opportunity to learn and grown personally and professionally
Evaluating the potential impact and benefits of taking a GAP year experience
Addressing the financial issues related to gap year expenses

Reviewing the GAP year's performance and progress.

Benefits

1. **Builds** character.

2. **Exposes** a young person to a different way of life.

3. **Enters** college with more perspective and maturity, and "slightly more" wisdom. [1]

Princeton encourages it; Harvard is a big fan of it. Tufts to MIT, some of the most prestigious universities in the nation are urging students to consider a taking a GAP year.

My GAP Year Proposal

Worksheet

Reasons for taking a GAP Year: ______________________________

____

____

GAP Year Goal: ______________________________

____

____

GAP Year Objectives:

1. ______________________________

2. ______________________________

3. ______________________________

GAP Year Plan: ______________________________

____

____

____

____

____

____

____

____

Targeted date for returning to school: ______________________________

Preparing For College and My Career

Stage III -Preparation

By failing to prepare, you are preparing to fail. **Benjamin Franklin**

Preparing for a career in today's rapidly changing, complex and highly technical marketplace has become a challenging and costly task for high school students and their parents. The objectives of the Evaluation Stage are to provide you with the opportunity to think through realistic career options available and confidently make wise decisions. Today's high school students are asking the following questions:

> **C**arla, a sophomore, said that she wanted to become a doctor, and asked, "What specific things should my parents and I look for as we review what school I should consider attending?"
>
> **O**liver, a senior, said, "I do not know what to look for in a college," and asked, "What should I look for in a college?"
>
> **L**arry, a junior, said, "My parents want me to go to their college, but I want to select my own college," and asked, "How do I respectfully convince them?"
>
> **L**inda, a senior, said, "My parents and I are wondering how we are going to pay for my college expenses," and asked, "What are our options?"
>
> **E**dward, a sophomore, asked, "What should I look for in a community college?"
>
> **G**eorge, a junior, asked, "How do my parents and I plan and prepare for college?"
>
> **E**llen, a senior, asked, "Since I am not interested in going to college, what are my options?"

What makes these more challenging questions to answer is the tremendous number of options available to students like you today; escalating college costs; and the rapidly changing educational, economic and technical environment? With the sound career process in progress, the next step is to begin exploring, evaluating and selecting realistic school options. The goal of the Preparation stage is to take the necessary steps to choose the school that best fits your personality and educational requirements, and that can effectively prepare you for your chosen career and the changing and competitive marketplace.

In choosing a school that will best prepare you for your career; you will need to answer: "What are the school's objectives? What types of schools exist?" and "What are the key criteria in selecting the right school?

> **School's objectives** should be to prepare students for their selected career and to enter the competitive marketplace.

Types of schools include vocational/technical, 2-year community colleges and 4-year colleges/universities (accredited or non-accredited, private or public, Christian or non-Christian).

Key criteria in considering and selecting a school should include their accreditation, educational purpose, philosophy and programs.

There are more than 3600+ colleges in the United States alone and many more internationally. Exploring and evaluating the right school to attend can be a complex and confusing process.

Thus, in reviewing your options, you first must review what the selected career educational requirements are; secondly review if the school can prepare you for your selected major and, finally, determine what the school's environment is like.

What are the career's requirements?

1. What type of personality, aptitude, abilities and skills do I need in order to be successful in my chosen career?

2. What courses, diplomas, degrees, and experience will I need to prepare for my chosen career?

3. Do I have the ability, dedication and motivation to satisfy all of training and experience requirements to prepare for my chosen field?

Will the school prepare me for my selected major?

1. What kind of guidance and internship programs does the school offer?

2. What is the school's record of graduates securing jobs within their career after graduation?

3. What is the school's reputation in Christian and non-Christian communities?

What is the school's environment like?

1. Will it be an academically challenging atmosphere enabled the further development of critical thinking and wise decision-making skills?

2. Will it be as supportive or hostile to my personal and spiritual life?

3. Will the school's regulations foster or hinder the development of social responsibility?

My Seven Key Criteria I Am Looking For in a College

Worksheet

Criteria#1:____

____

____

Criteria#2:____

____

____

Criteria#3:____

____

____

Criteria#4:____

____

____

Criteria#5:____

____

____

Criteria#6:____

____

____

Criteria#7:____

____

____

What Should I be looking for in a College?

Criteria Guidelines

Now that you have begun identifying and exploring potential schools to attend, it is time to begin reviewing the list of criteria of what to look for in a school, the school's admission guidelines and identification process.

List of Criteria

- Accreditation status
- Educational purpose and philosophy
- Reputation with Christian and non-Christian communities, graduates, employers, etc.
- Size of student enrollment and classes
- Location - rural, city; and climate
- Campus size, appearance and security
- Academic programs and calendar (two semesters, three terms or four quarters)
- Diploma and degree programs (One-Year Certificate, Associates, Bachelors)
- Admissions policies-US and international students
- Default rate
- Faculty-student ratio
- Academic advisement program
- Career planning, internship and job placement programs
- Student employment opportunities - US and international students
- Tuition, room and board, fees
- Financial aid program for U.S. and international students
- International co-op studies program
- Extracurricular activities, sports, music, Christian services, etc.
- Insurance and health services
- Housing size, quality, atmosphere and regulations
- Support services and systems for US and international students
- Community and cultural activities and opportunities

Admission Guidelines: Colleges and universities use the following admission criteria in evaluating their applicants for admission:

1. Academic record, which includes grades, class rank, subjects taken and types of courses, taken (regular, accelerated, advanced placement).

2. Test Scores - SAT & II - (Scholastic Aptitude Test), ACT - (American College Test) and Advanced Placement.

3. Extracurricular Activities show a record of commitment and involvement in school, church, and community.

4. Achievements in academic extracurricular and leadership fields.

5. Recommendation letters from teachers, counselors, and adults who know you well. These letters should include new insights about you not included in your application.

6. The Essay explaining reasons for your college selection educational and career goals, how you would benefit from attending their school, and what potential contribution you can make to the school.

7. Admission interview with admissions personnel.

Identification Process: You will need to complete the following steps when beginning identifying potential colleges of interest:

1. **Identify** and **list** three colleges of interest. **Key:** Do not limit your options to certain colleges.

2. **Send** an Information Request Letter to those colleges of interest and under consideration.

3. **Review** each of the college's websites and the other following web site for additional information about the colleges under consideration.

   a. College Board web site: www.collegeboard.com

   b. Christian Colleges: www.christiancolleges.com

Sample Information Request Letter

James Robinson
Apartado 29
Santa Angles, Bolivia
South America
robinsonj@aol.com

April 19, 2013

Mr. Mark Morgan
Admissions Office
Value University
250 Value Blvd
Value, TX 75660

Dear Mr. Morgan:

I am a junior attending Santa Angles High School, Santa Angles, Bolivia. I am an American citizen and will be graduating from high school in June 2007. My intended major is International Business with an emphasis in marketing.

I am interested in attending Value University, please send and would appreciate it if you would mail the following materials:

A catalog
An application form
Financial aid forms

Thank you for your kind assistance with this matter. I look forward to hearing from you soon.

Sincerely yours,

James Robinson

James Robinson

My List of Colleges under Consideration

Worksheet

1. **Identify** and **list** three potential colleges you are considering.

2. **Contact** the admission counselor you will be sending the letter. Pay attention to make sure you have the correct spelling of the counselor's name. It is just common courtesy; no one likes to have his or her name misspelled, and it leaves a poor impression.

3. **Write** a draft of your request letter. As a guide only, see sample information request letter in this guide. **Please do not just copy and use the sample letter!**

My List of Colleges

College #1: Admission Counselor's Name: ______________________________

College: ____

Address: ____

City: ______________________________ State: __________ Zip: ________

Phone Number: ____________________ Fax: ____________________

E-mail: ________________________ Website: ____________________

College #2: Admission Counselor's Name: ______________________________

College: ____

Address: ____

City: ______________________________ State: __________ Zip: ________

Phone Number: ____________________ Fax: ____________________

E-mail: ________________________ Website: ____________________

College #3: Admission Counselor's Name: ___________________________________

College: ____

Address:____

City:____________________________________ State: __________ Zip:________

Phone Number: __________________________ Fax: ____________________________

E-mail: ________________________________ Website: __________________________

Notes

____

____

____

____

____

____

____

____

____

____

____

____

____

Applying for College

Package & Process

Those who have completed the college application process have found it to be complex, competitive and costly process. **Complex** in the amount of forms and tests to be completed, documents to be submitted and deadlines to be met. **Competitive** in the large number of applications colleges receive for the limited numbers of openings, and **costly** with the various and numerous fees required for each application submitted. This complex, competitive and costly process only creates frustration and stress and makes no promises or warranties. To reduce frustration and stress in the application process it is essential to consider what is included in the application package and review the admission process and decision stages.

College Application Package typically includes the following items for US citizens and international students:

US Citizens

a. College application forms can be completed online.

b. Application fee that is usually non-refundable. Many colleges offer fee waivers for applicants from low-income households.

c. High School Transcript request form are filled out by the guidance office or the registrar.

d. Letters of Recommendations from teachers, counselors or other adults who know the prospective student well.

e. An essay that may include an autobiographical statement or a specific theme.

f. Interviews may be required.

g. Audition/Portfolio for students who are applying for music, art or design programs.

International Students

In addition to the items listed above are additional items for international students:

a. International Student Application and fees

b. College essay

c. TOEFL, SAT or ACT scores.

d. Official copies of secondary/high school record, indicating grades earned and examination results (if applicable), showing grades earned.

e. Official explanation of grading system.

f. Certified translations of any non-English certificates, diplomas, transcripts, and other documents submitted.

g. Completed Sponsor Statement Form and Bank Statement

The Admission Review Process includes:

The admissions advisor assigned to your high school is responsible for the initial review and evaluation of your academic and personal information presented in the application. The advisor will then submit your application with his comments, recommendation, and score to a senior level staff member for their review. Your application will receive a comprehensive score of one to five, with five being the highest. The score is based in the areas of academic and extracurricular achievements; degree of difficulty in high school curriculum; recommendation letters; essay; and personality qualities. Once the admission advisor and senior staff level member have completed their evaluation of your application, it is forwarded to the admissions committee for final their discussion and decision whether to accept, defer or deny your admission.

The goal of the college's admissions review process is to identify and admit students who are prepared to excellence the college challenging academic environment. Admit students who demonstrate strong academic achievements, the broad diversity of talents, experience, backgrounds and potential intellectual and cultural contributions that they can bring to college.

The Admissions Decision Stages include:

Early Decision (Binding) is an accelerated application process in which students must complete and submit their application in November 1st. In most cases, students may receive a decision from their college by December or January. If accepted under early decision, the student has to make a commitment to accept or reject the accepted offer. If accepted, then the student is required to discontinue all other college applications. **Early Action (Non-Binding)** students may apply for early admission to the decision made by early spring whether to accept or reject an admission offer. For students considering early decision, it is essential to evaluate if the school is a good fit and have the confidence that it is a clear choice that closely matches their personal and major requirements. **Regular decision** is the normal application process by which students apply by the established deadline and receives an admission decision by April 1 of their senior year. Decide to accept or decline acceptance, should be made by the college's established deadline. Finally, **Deferred Decision** students may defer their admission into college by one year for various reasons such as completing a gap year or attending community college.

Tracking My College Application Progress

Chart

Admission Counselor's Name:____

College:_____________________________ ________________________________

Address:____

City:____ State: _________ Zip:_________

Phone Number:_________________________ Fax Number:______________________

E-mail Address:______________________ Web site Address:______________________

Items	**Date**
Request college information and application	
Application	
Early	
Regular	
Mailed	
Received by college	
Transcripts	
Requested	
Mailed	
Received by college	
Test Scores	
SAT	
ACT	
Mailed	
Received by college	
Recommendation Letters	
Letter #1: Person's Name:	

Letter #2: Person's Name:	
Letter #3: Person's Name:	
Essay	
First Draft	
Final Draft Completed	
Application	
Completed and copied.	
Mailed with application fee and supporting documents	
Confirm receipt of application received	
Interviews If Required	
Schedule college interview	
Schedule alumni interview	
Send Thank You notes to interviewers	
Financial Aid Forms	
Priority financial aid deadline	
Regular financial aid deadline	
Mail or electronically filed FAFSA	
Mail institutional aid form	
Mail state aid form	
Received Admission Letter	
Received Financial Aid Award Letter	
Final Action to be completed	
Send accepting or declining letter.	
If accepting admission, send required deposit	
Request final transcripts be sent to the school	

Remember: makes copies of all documents before sending them to the college.

Explaining Why I Want to Go to College

College Essay

In the previous chapter you reviewed what is included in the college application package, the admissions review process and stages. A substantive part of the college application package is the college essay that presents a personal and human touch to the application. It is essential to remember that colleges receive many more applications for admission with similar grades, test scores and recommendation letters than they can accept. Therefore, when writing your essay, it will provide you with the opportunity for you to display your unique personality demonstrate your writing, organizational and critical thinking skills and set you apart from all of the other applicants. A well-written essay is one that is insightful, thoughtful, and captivating in its content. A well-written essay is one that brings out the author's genuine personality, beliefs, thoughts and interests about the essay selected question or topic. The essay question may require you to select a theme about yourself, event, book, quotation, educational and/or career aspiration or answer a specific question. **It is critical to avoid being shallow and careless in writing your essay or answering the question.** In highly competitive colleges, admissions committee members will use your college essay to evaluate what makes your application stand out from all the other applications under consideration. Most admissions personnel rated college essays as **75% mediocre; 15% poor,** and **10% good to excellent**.

Before starting your essay, you should carefully review what should be the goal of your essay; what admissions committees **do** and **do not** want to read and what to **remember** before starting your essay.

The **goal** of your essay should be **to:**

Exhibit your genuine personality, feelings, ideas and interests

Showcase your writing, organizational and critical thinking skills

Structure your essay creatively and concisely

Articulate your college and career aspirations

Yield additional information not provided in your grades or in test scores.

The admissions committees **do** want to read essays **that:**

Reflects a genuine portrait of who you are,

Reveals your writing, organizational and critical thinking skills, and

Focuses on your career and college aspiration, and potential contributions you can bring to college.

The admissions committees **do not** want to review essays that:

Express complaints about your teachers, school, parents, lack of academic performance,

Exaggerate information about yourself, events and accomplishments in your life, and

Reads like a professionally written, copied or downloaded from the internet.

Remember that admissions committees can **easily**:

Detect essays professionally written, copied and downloaded from the internet

Distinguish if the applicant wrote his or her own essay or if a professional wrote it

Diagnose whether the essay complements or contradicts the applicant's verbal and written communication style.

Key things to remember you will find it will be extremely beneficial, when you write your own college essay, which will take time and effort. It will also allow you the opportunity to set yourself apart from other applicants. **Finally,** tailor your college essays to address the uniqueness of each college and their essay requirements.

Preparing for College Entrance Exams

The PSAT, SAT & ACT

Over the past several years on the SAT course, I have received a variety of responses from students have responded with a variety of emotions, from outright fear of the exam to overestimating or underestimating the importance of the PSAT, SAT, ACT, AP in the college application process. Having a clean and balanced perspective of college entrance exams, understanding their objectives, and preparing effectively for them can provide confidence to complete the chosen college entrance exam. Now take a look at what the PSAT, SAT, SAT II, ACT and Advance Placement exams are. How long are these tests and when should they be taken?

The Preliminary Scholastic Assessment Test/National Merit Scholarship Qualifying Test provides students with firsthand practice tests in preparation for the SAT. It also provides students with the opportunity to get into the National Merit Scholarship Program (11th grade). Program (11th grade). The 2 hours and 10 minute test measure the student's critical reading, math problem-solving and writing test taking abilities. The objectives for taking the test are to show you what is your strengths and weakness in each area; enter the competition for National Merit Scholarship and allow you to develop a study program to improve in those areas you are weak in before submitting the SAT. For information on the PSAT/NMSAQT go to:
http://professionals.collegeboard.com/testing/psat

The Scholastic **A**ssessment **T**est is a standardized test to determine the student's academic potential readiness for college. It is 3 hours and 45 minute test comprises of critical reading, writing and math sections. The purpose of the SAT is to assess how well an individual does on tests. It provides a college, faced with thousands of applications, with a common denominator in the screening application process. Each section is given a grade ranging from 200 to 800-point scale, for a possible total test score of 2400 points. Most students take the SAT in during the spring of junior year or in the fall of their senior year in high school. Students who also take the test twice tend to improve their score the second time around. For additional information on the SAT go to: http://sat.collegeboard.org/home

The SAT Subject Tests determine the student's knowledge in some twenty-subject areas. It is taken to assist students' improve their application for admission. A student selects the subject they want to test in based on their college application requirements. It is a 1-hour exam, includes multiple-choice questions and an essay, and given a score ranging from 200 to 800 degrees. It is recommended that students complete their subject test right after finishing the course. It is completed in the spring of the junior year or fall of the senior year in high school. For additional information on the SAT Subject Tests go to: http://sat.collegeboard.org/register/

It is another common denominator that colleges use in screening their applicants. It is 3-hours and 30-minute test, which includes English, mathematics, reading, and science sections. A composite score between 1 (low) and 36 (high) is given based on the average of 4 scored sections. It should be taken in the spring of the junior year or fall of the senior year. Many colleges and universities accept the ACT; it is essential to check with the college or university which test they require you to take. For specific information on the ACT go to www.actstudent.org

The Advanced **P**lacement college-level courses and exams, students can earn college credits, advanced placement or both from most colleges and universities in the United States and more than 60 countries. AP courses and exams offered in 34 subjects. AP exam scores are reported in a range from 1 – not recommended to 5 – extremely well qualified point scale. In considering completing an AP course and exam, the following steps should be taken. The first step is to check with your AP teacher or coordinator for qualification, policy and process requirements. Any home schooled students or attend a school does not offer AP, should contact a participating school or check if your state sponsors online AP courses. The next step is to check with the college/university you are considering about their AP application, policy and procedures. For detailed and updated information, AP courses, exams, testing, registrations and fees information go to http://www.collegeboard.com/student/testing/ap/about.html

Summary

To prepare successfully for your chosen college entrance exams, you should review the following four steps:

1. **Placing** the PSAT, SAT and ACT exam in proper perspective, and remember they are merely one factor in the college application. **Key Point**: Do not overestimate or underestimate their importance.

2. **Identifying** what your verbal and mathematics strengths and weaknesses are and begin working on improving those weak areas

3. **Registering** to take and complete SAT or ACT preparation course prior to your scheduled testing date.

4. **Completing** an SAT or ACT Question of the Day via the following links:

   SAT - http://sat.collegeboard.org/practice/sat-question-of-the-day
   http://www.number2.com/exams/sat/daily/question/index.cfm
   ACT - http://www.actstudent.org/qotd/

My Perception College Entrance Exams

Worksheet

1. Do you have any of your own relaxation techniques that you use before taking a test? ______

____

____

2. What does it mean to keep things positive while taking a test? ________________________

____

____

3. What can you do to maintain focus when taking a test?______________________________

____

____

4. Do you have any problems in concentrating on taking a test and if so how do you deal with it.

____

____

5. What does it mean by keeping the SAT in proper perspective? ________________________

____

____

6. What attitude, feelings and thoughts come to mind when you think of taking the SAT? _____

____

____

7. When taking a test, who is in control, you or the test? ______________________________

____

Paying for College

The What, When and How!

One of the most critical issues facing today's college-bound students and their parents is the escalating cost of higher education. The average cost of a four-year public college is currently $43,000+ and a four-year private college averages $110, 000+. What is even more alarming is that only 25% of undergraduate students complete college in four years. The majority of today's students finish college in 5 to 7 years due to changing their majors several times, requiring an increase in the number of years to fulfill their degree requirements and the rising cost of college. With the educational selection process completed, the next step is identifying types of financial aid programs and the application procedures. Take the following steps when addressing financial aid matters:

Pray for God's wisdom and guidance, on how to plan and prepare for those anticipated college expenses;

Plan a strategy to identify potential sources of financial aid; and

Prepare to complete financial aid applications ahead of set deadlines.

The first critically step in the financial aid process is the culmination of the FAFSA! No one will be considered for any financial aid without it!

The following are three key sources of financial aid:

Public Programs

The first key source of financial aid provided is through the federal and state governments. These include the following:

1. **Pell Grants** are awarded to undergraduate students earning a bachelor's or professional degree. They provide a basis for which other aid may be added. For updated and other information on the Pell Grant go to: http://www2.ed.gov/programs/fpg/index.html

2. **Federal Family Educational Opportunity Grants** (FFEOG) are based on the student's financial needs. For additional and updated information on the FFEOG go to: http://www2.ed.gov/programs/fseog/index.html

3. **Federal Family Educational Opportunity Grants** (FFEOG) are based on the student's financial needs. For additional and updated information on the FFEOG go to: http://www2.ed.gov/programs/fseog/index.html

4. **Stafford Subsidized Loans** are for students with financial need; the student will not be charged interest during the authorized deferment period. The government subsidizes the interest on the loan during the deferment period. For additional and updated information go to: http://studentaid.ed.gov/PORTALSWebApp/students/english/index.jsp

5. **Stafford Unsubsidized Loans** are for students without financial need and the interest charges start from the time the loan is disbursed to the student. http://studentaid.ed.gov/PORTALSWebApp/students/english/index.jsp

6. **Direct Plus Loans** are for parents. For updated and additional information on Direct Plus Loan http://www.direct.ed.gov/parent.html

7. **Federal Perkins Loans** are low interest, campus-based loan programs. Go to http://www2.ed.gov/programs/fpl/index.html for additional and updated information on the Federal Perkins Loan.

8. **Federal Work Study** provides students with employment opportunities to earn money to pay for their educational expenses. This program encourages working while in college. For updated and detailed information on the work study program go to www2.ed.gov/programs/fws/index.html

9. **Consolation Loan Programs** provide students and their parents with the opportunity to consolidate various federal educational loans into one loan. For updated and additional information on consolidating loans go to: http: /student aid. Ed. Gov/PORTALSWebApp/students/English/consolidation.jsp? tab=repaying

10. **The Loan Cancellation Program** provides students with the opportunity to serve in low-income areas for five consecutive years after college. For specific and updated information on the Cancellation Program go to: www.direct.ed.gov/cancellation.html

11. **E**ducational **A**ssistance **P**artnership **P**rogram is a federal and state partnership program.

11. **Tax Credits** such as the:

    The Child Tax Credit, a credit, enables parents to take $500+ off their tax bill for each child they support. To qualify the child must be less than 17 at the end of the year and a U.S. citizen. The child tax credit reduces as income increases.

The Lifetime Learning Credit is a tax credit equal to 20% of the post-secondary tuition paid each year. The maximum credit per tax return is $1, 000 per year.

The Hope Scholarship Credit is a tax credit per student per year for the first two years of the student's post-secondary education.

To claim Hope Scholarship Credit, you must be enrolled in a qualified recognized educational program, leading to a degree or diploma. For the latest legislative changes and updates on the Hope Scholarship Tax Credit go to www.finaid.org/otheraid/hopescholarship.phtml

Lifetime Learning Credit for students enrolled in a qualifying educational institution. For more and updated information on the lifetime learning credit, go to www.studentaid.com/Paying/Tax-Aid/Lifetime-Learning-Credit

Saving for College has become intimidating and difficult due to a large number of financial saving programs available and potential limited incomes for many families today. To evaluate the best savings options, for your particular financial situation, you should complete two following steps. First, review the list of all qualifying saving programs available by reviewing the SmartStudent Guide to Financial Aid www.finaid.org/savings/. After reviewing the list of saving programs available; contact and discuss your best options with a qualified financial planning advisor.

The Key point regarding tax credits is that they are constantly changing. Keeping informed of these changes is essential.

The Guide to Federal Student Aid provides a description of grants, loans, and work-study aid available from the Department's Federal Student Aid office. The annually updated guide is available from the Federal Student Aid Information Center at 1-800-433-3243 or online http://studentaid.ed.gov/students/publications/student_guide/index.html

12. Military Programs include:

United Stat Air Force Academy - http://www.usafa.af.mil/
Naval Academy - http://www.usna.edu/homepage.php
West Point - http://www.usma.edu/
Marine Academy - http://www.marines.com/home

The military academy application process to:
http://www.whitehouse.gov/administration/vice-president-biden/academy-nominations/steps

ROTC Scholarships are a four-year Air Force, Army and Naval s Scholarships Program. High School students are awarded based on a national competition. Each year 4,000 winners are awarded scholarships to 4,000 out of 25,000 applicants. Recipients of the scholarships must commit to serve in the military in the branch of their choice.

The US Armed Forces Recruiting Program provides Montgomery GI Bill and other college savings programs for individuals who serve in the military for a specific number of years.

13. State Programs vary from state to state. To qualify for public financial aid, grants, work-study and loans, you must be a U.S. citizen or an eligible non-citizen student, have a valid Social Security number; and register with the Selective Service (males18-25). You required receiving a high school diploma, GED Certificate or a test approved by the Department of Education. You will need to enroll in an accredited or certificate program as a regular student working toward a degree or certificate, maintain satisfactory academic progress, and demonstrate financial need.

Finally, you required to sign a statement on the FAFSA certifying that federal aid will be for educational purposes and that you are not in default on any federal student loans.

Important Point to Remember: Students convicted of the sale or possession of drugs will be ineligible (one year from the date of their first conviction, two years after their second conviction, and indefinitely after a third conviction) for federal financial aid. http://www.sss.gov

Private Programs are grants and scholarships provided by foundations, companies, etc.

Institutional Programs are the college's unique and distinct in-house financial aid packages, offered to students who have been accepted at their school. Examples include prepaid tuition, work/study, grants, loans and institutional scholarships.

Scholarships are a component of the financial aid package. Several types of scholarships are awarded to support the student's education and are based on the student's various achievements. In applying for scholarships, it is essential to be aware of and review the myths about scholarships, scholarship scams common mistakes made and procedures in searching for and completing scholarship applications

Scholarships Myths: The following are 7 myths about scholarships:

Myth 1: Billions of scholarship dollars go unclaimed.

Myth 2: I cannot possibly get a scholarship because of the stiff competition.

Myth 3: Scholarships require a glamorous talent.

Myth 4: Scholarship searches are worth paying for.

Myth 5: Scholarships go only to the best students.

Myth 6: I am a top student, so I do not have to seek scholarships. They will come to me.

Myth 7: If I apply for a loan, it will lessen my chances for a scholarship.

Seven Scholarships Scams: The Federal Trade Commission urges students and parents to watch for the following signs that a college scholarship offer is a scam.

1. Invitation to attend a free seminar about scholarships.

2. The scholarship is guaranteed or your money back.

3. You cannot find this information anywhere else.

4. We will need your credit card or bank account number to hold this scholarship.

5. We will do all the work for you.

6. The scholarship will cost some money.

7. You have been selected by a "national foundation" to receive a scholarship or "You're a finalist" in a contest you never entered.

Scholarship Procedures: In identifying and searching for scholarships the following strongly suggest steps to take.

1. **Realize** that you have to perform the work yourself.

2. **Complete** the PSAT, SAT and/or ACT; they are sources of thousands of National Merit Scholarships.

3. **Complete** a FAFSA (Free Application for Federal Student Aid) is the key to obtaining about 70% of federal student aid.

4. **Check** out the following scholarship web sites:

   Fast WEB: www.fastweb.com

   College Board:
   www.collegeboard.org/index-this/fundfinder/html/sschtop.html
   National Merit Scholarship Corporation: www.nationalmerit.org

   Sallie Mae's Online Scholarship Service:
   www.scholarships.salliemae.com

   College Parents of America: www.collegeparents.org

5. **Complete** an online student profile form from the following websites. You will find a listing of scholarships that match your profile.

   www.collegeboard.com

   www.wiredscholar.com

6. **Contact** high school guidance counselor and college financial aid office for additional sources. Observe carefully the guidelines and deadlines when completing financial aid applications.

7. **Continue** to pray for guidance in searching for new scholarship opportunities.

Scholarship Mistakes: The following are 7 most common mistakes made by students and their parents:

1. **Filling** out the FAFSA application incorrectly and late.

2. **Saving** in your child's name.

   Students are expected to contribute **35%** of their savings/assets to college expenses.

   Parents are expected to contribute **5.64%** of their assets to college expenses.

3. **Sending** in forms too late waiting until the last minute.

4. **Paying** a consultant to assist in filling out the financial aid forms.

5. **Reading** the wrong bottom line total college expenses vs financial aid package.

6. **Passing** up the chance to negotiate for additional aid.

7. **Incomplete** budget leaving out non-educational expenses (travel home, social activities, etc.).

Additional Resources

1. *Scholarship Myths* – www.FastWeb.org

2. *Scholarship Scams* – www.FinAid.org

3. *How to Avoid Scholarship Scams.* www.FinAid.org

My List of College Contacts Information

Chart

School #1

College's Name

Address

City, State Zip

Contact's Name

Phone # Fax#

E-mail address

Web Site Address

Potential Major

Application Deadline

School #2

College's Name

Address

City, State Zip

Contact's Name

Phone # Fax#

E-mail address

Web Site Address

Potential Major

Application Deadline

Projected Expenses	
Tuition & Fees	$
Room & Board	$
Books & Supplies	$
Transportation	$
Personal	$
Other:	$
	$
Total (Yearly)	$
Expected Family Contribution	$
Estimated Financial Aid Needed	$

Projected Expenses	
Tuition & Fees	$
Room & Board	$
Books & Supplies	$
Transportation	$
Personal	$
Other:	$
	$
Total (Yearly)	$
Expected Family Contribution	$
Estimated Financial Aid Needed	$

Comparing My College Options

Chart

School #1: ____________________	School #1: ____________________
____________________	____________________
Accreditation status	Accreditation status
____________________	____________________
____________________	____________________
____________________	____________________
Educational purpose and philosophy	Educational purpose and philosophy
____________________	____________________
____________________	____________________
____________________	____________________
Reputation	Reputation
____________________	____________________
____________________	____________________
____________________	____________________
Size of student enrolment and classes	Size of student enrolment and classes
____________________	____________________
____________________	____________________
____________________	____________________
Location - rural, suburban, urban and climate	Location - rural, suburban, urban and climate
____________________	____________________
____________________	____________________

Campus size, appearance and security	Campus size, appearance and security
Academic programs	Academic programs
Diploma and degree programs	Diploma and degree programs
Admissions policies	Admissions policies
Default rate	Default rate
Faculty-student ratio	Faculty-student ratio
Academic advisement program	Academic advisement program

Career planning, internship, job placement programs, & student employment opportunities	Career planning, internship, job placement programs, & student employment opportunities
______________________	______________________
______________________	______________________
______________________	______________________
Tuition, room and board, fees	Tuition, room and board, fees
______________________	______________________
______________________	______________________
______________________	______________________
Academic Environment	Academic Environment
______________________	______________________
______________________	______________________
______________________	______________________
Financial Aid Program	Financial Aid Program
______________________	______________________
______________________	______________________
______________________	______________________
International co-op studies program	International co-op studies program
______________________	______________________
______________________	______________________
______________________	______________________
Extracurricular activities	Extracurricular activities
______________________	______________________
______________________	______________________

Insurance and health services	Insurance and health services
Housing size, quality, atmosphere and regulations	Housing size, quality, atmosphere and regulations
Support services and systems	Support services and systems
Community and cultural activities & opportunities	Community and cultural activities & opportunities
Others	Others
Overall Evaluation	**Overall Evaluation**

My College Evaluation and Selection

Chart

Criteria	School # 1	School # 2
Accreditation		
School's purpose and philosophy		
Reputation		
Size of student enrollment and classes		
Location		
Campus size, appearance and security		
Academic program and calendar		
Degree programs		
Admissions policy		
Default rate		
Teaching Faculty - student ratio		
Advisement program		
Guidance and job placement programs		
Student employment opportunities		
Tuition and fees		
Financial aid programs		
International co-op program		
Extracurricular program		
Insurance and health services		
Housing size, appearance, atmosphere and regulations		
Support services and system		
Community and cultural activities and opportunities		
An academic environment		
Total		
Divided by 23		
Overall Rating		

Rating System: 1 is below 2-meets and **3 exceeds my expectations**

Managing My Money Wisely

Money Management 101

During the last decade, the role of paying for college shifted from parents to the students. Consequently, more students are opting for student loans than ever before. Today, over 60% of all financial aid is a government-backed student or parent loans, and as prices continue to rise, student borrowing continues to escalate as well. Student loans are not the problem. The problem is students, who borrow in excess of what they need to get a college education. [1]

Did you know that?

> *Excessive Credit Card Use Causes Student Debt Woes* – Jamie Barrett, Kansas State Collegian
>
> *Many college students are not only leaving school with diplomas, but also the unmanageable debt burdens* – CNN/Money
>
> *Student debt on the rise – More student are graduating with larger debt burdens a part of their fiscal future* – CNN/Money
>
> *An Alert to the Dangers of Student Debt* – Michelle Singletary, Washington Post

Debt has become such an enormous issue for both students and their parents because students:

> **D**ecide to take out loans without considering the serious implications for their future personal, professional and financial future**...**
>
> **E**ncouraged to take out educational loans by federal, state and college officials
>
> **B**uy desired and unnecessary products and services with credit cards to satisfying their unchecked consumerism
>
> **T**ake credit cards without understanding the credit card's terms and their implications on their credit rating.

For students desiring to graduate with the least amount of debt require the development money skills. Money management skills that require:

> **Dedicating** yourself not to get into deep debt through the overuse of credit cards and loans.
>
> **Determining** what your needs, wants, and desires are.

Needs are the purchases necessary to provide your basic requirements such as food, clothing, home, medical coverage, and others.

Wants involve choices about the quality of goods to be used, such as dress clothes versus work clothes, steak versus hamburger, or a new car versus a used car.

Desires are choices that are made only out of the surplus funds after all other obligations have been met.

Developing a monthly budget plan to:

1. **Track** income and expenses.

2. **Avoid** financial bondage by eliminating potential impulsive purchases on credit.

3. **Have** the freedom to pursue personal and professional goals.[2]

My Projected Monthly Budget

Chart

Income	
Salary	
Savings and checking interests	
Scholarships & Loans	
Parents	
Other	
Total:	
Minus	
Tithes	
Taxes	
Total Available Income:	
Expenses	
Room and board	
Linen and supplies	
Telephone	
Utilities	
Tuition and fees	
Computer	
Repair	
Supplies	
Internet Service	
Printer	
Supplies	
Books and supplies	
Automobile	
Insurance	

License & Taxes	
Gas and oil	
Repairs	
Travel	
Clothing	
Laundry and dry cleaning	
New clothing purchases	
Medical	
Insurance	
Doctor	
Dentist	
Prescriptions	
Debts Payments	
School loans	
Regular Loans	
Credit Cards	
Personal	
Cosmetics/Saving/Haircuts	
Fraternity/Sorority	
Supplies	
Entertainment	
Dinner	
Social activities	
Dates	
Trips	
Others	
Total Income:	
Total Monthly Expenses:	
Balance Available:	

Identifying the Quality and Strength of My Character

Character's Foundation

Over the past decades we have seen the economic, social, political and technical foundations being shattered by tornados, hurricanes, floods, earthquakes and tsunami.

Tornados causing massive changes in the economic, social, political, and technical landscape, impacting all levels of government, business and workforce.

Hurricanes destroying and creating new businesses, changing the way they operate and shortening the lifespan of products and services being offered.

Floods of cheap imports and the rising demands of the cost-conscious consumer for quality service and products at a fair price.

Earthquakes shattering businesses and the average worker's dreams, aspirations, goals and objectives, with major organizations filing for bankruptcy due to unethical business practices or foreign competition and the replacement of long-term, high-paying benefits jobs with benefits with short-term, low-paying non-benefited jobs.

Tsunami shifting the moral standards of right and wrong to the amoral gray area

To prepare for and manage a satisfying career that honors God in today's confusing, competitive and changing global marketplace requires that your career be built and maintained on a solid and strong foundation that will withstand job market tornados, hurricanes, floods, earthquakes and tsunami. A foundation that is constructed and maintained on **Godly**:

Trust: Trust in the Lord with all your heart, and lean not on your own understanding; in all your ways acknowledge him and he will make your paths straight. **Proverbs 3:5-6**

Assurance: For I know the plans I have for you," declares the Lord, "plans to prosper you and not to harm you, plan to give you a hope and a future. **Jeremiah 29:11**

Strength: I can do everything through him who gives me strength. **Philippians 4:13**

God desires that your personal and professional foundation include the following four cornerstones

1. **Uncompromising Ethics:** *He whose walk is blameless and who does what is righteous, who speaks the truth from his heart.* ***Psalm 15:2***

2. **Eternal Values**: *Whatever you do, work at it with all your heart, as working for the Lord, not for men, since you know that you will receive an inheritance from the Lord as a reward. It is the Lord Christ you are serving.* ***Colossians 3:23-24***

3. **Realistic Goals:** *Suppose one of you wants to build a tower. Will he not first sit down and estimate the cost to see if he has enough money to complete it? For if he lays the foundation and is not able to finish it, everyone who sees it will ridicule him, saying, "This fellow began to build and was not able to finish."* ***Luke 14:29***

4. **Proper Perspective on Success:** *"Well done, good and faithful servant! You have been faithful with a few things; I will put you in charge of many things. Come and share your master's happiness."* ***Matthew 25: 23***

Identifying and Understanding Ethics

Ethics 101

Did you read or hear that?

A Cheating Crisis in America's Schools - A Crisis in America's Schools — How It's Done and Why It's Happening – **ABC Primetime Special**

Poll: Majorities See Widespread Corruption - **ABC News**

Corruption deprives millions of access to essential healthcare. - **TI's Global Corruption Report**

"Today's ethical foundation is rapidly decaying by the widespread compromise of morals and the disappearance of the distinguishing line between right and wrong. Our educational system has long since abandoned the teaching of morals or what is now called in academia "value judgments." Absolutes of right and wrong have largely disappeared and have been replaced by a fuzzy, gray fog of inconsistent moral choices. Contempt and disregard for the law have become chronic. Many in our society obey laws only when it fits their agenda conveniently. Obedience to the law and to a set of absolute values greater than ourselves has taken a back seat to personal gain and situational ethics. There is a sullen cynicism in the air, so pervasive that Harvard University Sociologist David Riesman has warned that Americans are approaching the point where the prevailing ethic is "You're a fool to follow the rules."[4] Situational ethics and competitive compromise causes many to go the route of personal and professional prostitution, selling their souls for the sake of success. [3]

Ethics is a set of moral principles, the moral navigator of the conscience, the Revealer of the character's moral state, and the identifier of one's values. Ethics encompasses the broad science or teaching of how to live a life of integrity in the context of one's society or culture. It incorporates the accepted standards of the community as well as the personal conduct of an individual in that community. It is essential to define what ethics is, identify its key ingredients and standards and review ethics' relevance in your personal and professional life.

Definition of ethics is a set of moral principles, the moral navigator of the conscience, the Revealer of the character's moral state, and the identifier of one's values. It encompasses the science and teaching of how to live and act.

Ingredients of ethics or integrity, the state of wholeness, consistency and sincerity, with no deception or pretense. Honesty, the absence of lies, crookedness, deceit or fraud. Honesty is truthfulness, sincerity and frankness. Conscience, the inner compass that helps navigate the moral areas of life. [4]

Standards - It is God's desire for your private and public life exhibits the following qualities in your character:

a. **Integrity** – *Better a poor man whose walk is blameless than a rich man whose ways are perverse. (Proverbs 28:6) It teaches us to say "No" to ungodliness and worldly passions, and to live self-controlled, upright and godly lives.* ***Titus 2:12***

b. **Honesty** -*Whatever is true, whatever is noble, whatever is right, whatever is pure, and whatever is lovely, whatever is admirable – if anything is excellent or praiseworthy think about such things.* ***Philippians 4:8***

c. **Conscience** -*Fulfilling our responsibilities with a clear conscience, sincere heart and reverence for the Lord.* ***Colossians 3:23-24***

Identifying what is Important to Me

Values 102

Values are the second cornerstone of one's foundation. In reviewing and evaluating the values cornerstone, the questions you will begin to ask and answer are "How do I define my values and by whose standards?" "What are the key ingredients of my values?" "What impact do my values have on my personal and professional life?"

Definition

Values are standards by which you measure what is important and worthwhile in your life. They are a:

1. **Reflection** of your ethical standards and character

2. **Measurement** of what is important in your life

3. **Guide** to your decision-making process

4. **Factors** that give birth to your goals

Standards

God calls you to exhibit the following values in your attitude and actions

> "As Christians our values must be biblically based if we are to reclaim our minds for Christ. Whereas some values are a matter of preference, such as choosing books over sports, other values are absolute and clearly taught in Scripture.
>
> In direct contrast to our culture's values, authentic Christian values regard people above possessions, others above self, righteousness above the temporary pleasure of sin, His will above my will, forgiveness above revenge, giving above receiving, children above careers, character above credentials, truth above falsehoods, fact above feeling, commitment above comfort, and Christ above culture. Because our values determine how we organize facts and drive us towards decisions, clear Biblical values help guarantee a thought process that is godly, beneficial and eternally significant."[5]

Types

The following are three types of values we have in our lives:

Personal values are horizontal and apply to the individual personally and jointly with family and friends.

Professional values apply to and influence one's own college and career

Spiritual values are vertical ones that apply and impacts one's relationship with their God and horizontal impacting one's spiritual relationships with family, friends and church family.

Your values must be consciously identified, clarified and harmonized. If they do not complement each other, they can create stress in one's value system.

Listing My Values

Worksheet

Values	**Rating**
Obtaining wealth and an independent life	______
Developing a healthy family relationship	______
Promoting my life and career goals	______
Developing a character of integrity	______
Establishing life and career security	______
Being admired for who I am and my accomplishments	______
Being physically fit	______
Developing harmony between my spiritual, personal and professional life	______
Obtaining political power	______
Producing excellence in my college and career	______
Being creative	______
Serving my community	______
Taking risks	______
Being well paid for my work	______
Fulfilling my personal and professional potential	______
Obtaining status and fame in school, church, community or career	______
Having a challenging and satisfying career	______
Being unique in school and career	______
Having a variety of activities in my life.	______

Obtaining respect from my friends and fellow workers ______

Developing wisdom ______

Having a position of authority ______

Being in a competitive environment ______

Having good health ______

Having freedom and flexibility in my schedule ______

Developing financial security ______

Having personal and professional peace ______

Developing personally, educationally and professionally ______

Reaching my personal and professional goals ______

My three most important values are:

Value # 1 ______________________________ **Why:** ______________________

____

____

____

Value # 2 ______________________________ **Why:** ______________________

____

____

____

Value # 3 ______________________________ **Why:** ______________________

____

____

____

Where Am I Heading?

Stage IV – Goals

Your goals are the road maps that guide you and show you what is possible for your life.

Les Brown

Goals is the third cornerstone in one's character foundation. The majority of today's high school students enter college without any educational and career goals. They find themselves walking through the halls of academia without any direction, resulting in changing of their majors several times during their college years and completing college in five to seven years rather than four. Students who have some educational and career goals have greater motivation and commitment to their studies. Their college experience becomes purposeful, meaningful and rewarding. Now look at the definition of goals and objectives, and types of goals.

Goals are planned and purposefully directed efforts toward a specific destination. [1]

Objectives are clear and concise steps taken to achieve established goals. Therefore, as you are considering goals, you will need to test the validity of your goals by carefully reviewing and answering the following questions:

1. Are my goals realistic and reachable?

2. Have I established clear and concise objectives to accomplish my goals?

3. Are my goals relevant to who I am?

Types: Establishing goals require identifying the types and length of the goals you desire to set and establish objectives to reach them. The following are examples of short and long range personal, educational, and career goals and their objectives.

1. **Personal Long Term Goals** are specific things you want to accomplish in your lifetime,

   Goal – Become more like Christ

   Objectives – I will begin developing a more Christ like attitude in my thinking, attitude and actions by daily praying, reading and studying His word and memorizing verses.

2. **Personal Short Range Goals** are specific things you want to achieve.

   Goal - Lose weight

   Objectives – I will take two walks around the block each every day, watch what I eat, and develop a daily exercise program

3. **Educational Long-Range Goals** are a desired diploma, degree, professional certificates.

   Goal – Earn a BS in Electrical Engineering.

   Objectives - I will write to engineering schools requesting information on their engineering programs; I will research electrical engineering careers, and I will conduct information interviews with several electrical engineers.

4. **Educational Short Range Goals** are specific courses or projects to complete within a semester or academic year.

   Goal - Earn 4.0 in any Microeconomics Course

   Objectives - I will schedule a regular study period on microeconomics, and read additional resources on the topic

5. **Career Long Range Goals** are a list of accomplishments and positions you wish to attain.

   Goal - Become a high school principal at an international Christian school.

   Objectives - I will apply for a teaching position at a school in Germany, take professional education classes in school administration, and seek opportunities to assist in the administrative areas.

6. **Career Short Range Goals** are a list of professional projects you wish to accomplish in your job, new things you want to memorize, as well as professional skills you want to acquire.

   Goal - write a book.

   Objectives - I will schedule time each day to develop and write down my thoughts, ask several people to review my draft, and complete the final draft before sending it to the publisher.

In setting personal, educational and career goals, the apostle James strongly encourages you to remember the following:

> *Instead, you ought to say, if it is the Lord's will, we will live and do this or that* ***James 4:15.***

James reminds you that it is essential to include God in your goal setting process. Leaving Him out of this process could lead to failure and disappointment.

My List of Long and Short Term Goals

Chart

Short-term Personal Goals	**Dates**	**Long-term Personal Goals**	**Dates**
______________________	_____	______________________	_____
______________________	_____	______________________	_____
______________________	_____	______________________	_____
Short-term Educational Goals	**Dates**	**Long-term Educational Goals**	**Dates**
______________________	_____	______________________	_____
______________________	_____	______________________	_____
______________________	_____	______________________	_____
Short-term Career Goals	**Dates**	**Long-term Career Goals**	**Dates**
______________________	_____	______________________	_____
______________________	_____	______________________	_____
______________________	_____	______________________	_____

Identifying True Meaning of Success

Success 104

Don't aim for success if you want it; just do what you love and believe in, and it will come naturally.
David Frost

Success is the fourth and final cornerstone in one's character foundation. Success will mean different things to different people. To one person's success may mean being wealthy. To another individual it may mean having a happy and healthy family. To another person it may mean being happy with who they are and in their career. Your definition of success is based on the kind of ethics and values you have and the types of goals you want to set. Each cornerstone influences and impacts the other. The following are three definitions of success, the picture and principles of success and biblical perspective of what true success is.

Definition

Success is an achievement of something desired and planned.

Principles:

Seeing clearly God's definition and view of success – Colossians 3:23-24

Utilizing your God-given resources and responsibilities to its fullest potential - Matthew 25:14 - 28

Confident in your established college and career goals and objectives - Jeremiah 29:11

Searching opportunities to develop and manage a fulfilling career that honors God - Ecclesiastes 3:22

Seeing how God is using your personal and professional life to further His' eternal kingdom on earth - Matthew 6:19-20

Perspective

1. **Discovering** your God-given uniqueness and developing it to its fullest potential.

For you created my inmost being; you knit me together in my mother's womb. I praise you because I am fearfully and wonderfully made; your works are wonderful, I know that full well. My frame was not hidden from you when I was made in the secret place. When I was woven together in the depths of the earth, your eyes saw my unformed body. All the days ordained for me were written in your book before one of them came to be.

How precious to me are your thoughts, O God! How vast is the sum of them! Where I to count them, they would outnumber the grains of sand.

Psalm 139:13-18

2. **Having** a righteous, wise and discerning heart and an honorable reputation with God and man.

   So give your servant a discerning heart to govern your people and to distinguish between right and wrong. I will do what you asked. I will give you a wise and discerning heart, so that there will never have been anyone like you, nor will there ever be. ***1 Kings 3:9, 12***

3. **Pursing** a God-honoring and satisfying career, utilizing your personality and its unique characteristics in service to others.

   Then I realized that it is good and proper for a man to eat and drink, and to find satisfaction in his toilsome labor under the sun during the few days of life God has given him - for this is his lot. ***Ecclesiastes 5:18***

Lastly, it is necessary to remember that each cornerstone has an influence on one another. Your ethics determines your values. Your values determine what goals you set. Remember:

Your ethics + values + goals = your definition of success.

Finally, the strength and quality of your cornerstones reveal the strength and quality of your character's foundation.

Identifying the Quality and Strength of My Character

Worksheet

1. How important is it to have a solid and strong foundation?

____

____

____

2. On what should your foundation be established?

____

____

____

3. What are three reasons for building your foundation of God?

____

____

____

4. What roles do the four cornerstones play in building and maintaining a strong foundation during the career building process?

____

____

____

5. What impact do your ethics have upon you definition of your values?

____

____

____

6. What effect do your values have upon establishing your goals?

____

____

____

7. What impact do your goals have upon defining what success means to you?

____

____

____

8. What impact does God have or should He have in shaping your ethics, values, goals and definition of success?

____

____

____

9. Can you have a strong foundation when one or more of your cornerstones are weak?

____

____

____

Marketing Myself

Stage V – Campaign

No one can make you feel inferior without your consent **Eleanor Roosevelt**

Now that you have been working on identifying your **hand** – personality and its unique characteristics, and **glove** your career and college options, you can start the fifth stage of the career planning process, the College & Career Campaign. It is a logical plan with clear and concise goals and objectives to find the right college and career/job that is the right fit for you. For example, an **Educational Campaign** goal would be admitted to LeTourneau University's computer science program. A **Career Campaign** goal would be to be hired by Verizon as a computer systems analyst. Before you start working on your college and career campaign, you will need to review and answer the following questions:

1. What is your **uniqueness** that a potential college and/or employer should want to know about you?

2. What is your **passion** and how can it complement and enhance a potential college and the employer's own purpose and vision?

3. What are your **natural abilities** and **learned skills** that you possess that a college and the employer would desire?

4. What **relevant experience** do you have that a potential college and employers should know about and benefit from?

5. What **values** can you bring to a college and/or an employer that no one else can?

6. What are your **short** and **long-range goals** and can they complement and enhance your targeted college and/or employer's goals?

7. What makes you the **best choice** above your competitors for admission and/or employment?

You will notice that you have started answering these questions while completing your various parts of your career planning program. These above questions enable you to summarize what you have learned about yourself and prepare you in:

Develop a compelling personal brand statement to **capture** the college and/or employer's interest

Write an effective résumé and letter to **catch** an interviewer's attention

Implement effective networking strategies to **connect** with key decision makers

Conduct successful interviews to **compete** against your competition for admissions and employment.

Personal Brand

What is personal brand statement? It is a **captivating** and **memorable statement that you want others to see** and **remember about you**. It is used by well-known business, political and sports leaders. **Personal Brand is not** a job title, which an employer gives you. **Personal Brand** is a **captivating**, **creative, concise** and **solution-oriented statement** that **communicates who** you are, **what** you do best, **whom** you serve as illustrated by the following example:

John enables high school students, university students, professionals and businesses find answers to issues they are facing by asking a distinctive set of targeted questions leading to practical answers.

10 Steps to Developing a Personal Brand Statement

In creating your personal brand statement requires to take time to complete the following steps:

1. **Review** your personality indicator and list key attributes that make you unique.

2. **Review** your interest inventory and list your chosen career interest.

3. **Review** and list your passion, natural abilities and learned skills.

4. **Think** of what kind of personal brand image you want others to see and remember.

5. **Identify** what makes you unique and what you are good at.

6. **Identify** key targets you want to reach in your college and career campaign.

7. **Summarize** your key personal and professional attributes that make you who are you, what you are naturally good at and enjoy doing and who you enjoy working with.

8. **Write** a captivating, creative and solution-oriented sentence describing key elements of personal branding statement: The Who, Whom and What.

9. **Have** several trusted individuals who know you very well review and make recommendations with regard to your initial personal brand statement.

10. **Finalize** your authentic and captivity personal brand statement.

My Personal Brand Key Characteristics

1. Who ____

2. Whom ____

3. What ____

My Personal Brand Captivating Statement

____

____

____

The key point to remember is that for any college and career campaign to be effective and successful requires a captivating, creative and solution-oriented Personal Brand Statement as its foundation.

Employers have given the following reasons for not hiring individuals they have interviewed:

First, their lack of presenting a compelling personal brand statement/image, low self-confidence, ineffective résumé, weak interviewing skills, and unrealistic expectations

Second, their lack of preparation for the interview, inability to ask relevant questions, and an arrogant attitude

Third, their lack of presenting short-and long-term professional goals resulting in indecisiveness about one's career pursuits.

A college graduate called my office to schedule an appointment to discuss his lack of success in finding a job since graduating from college. I requested he come in with his resume and to dress as if he were attending a job interview. Several days later he came in for his mock interview in a T-shirt, jean and sneaker.

He handed me a handwritten resume. I asked him how long he had been searching for a job. His answer was two weeks. Harry shared about the interview he had with an airline in New Jersey.

He explained that the interviewer was interested in his background. He had expressed a desire to hire him as an accountant. Toward the end of the interview, the employer asked Harry one last question, "What are your short and long range career goals?" After thinking about the question, Harry responded, "I do not know." Within seconds, the interviewer said, "How do you expect us to hire you if you don't know where you are headed in your career?" The interviewer thanked him for coming in for the interview. Proper preparation, right attitude, and strategic resources will determine how long it will take for someone to reach their campaign's goal.

"Résumé" is the French word for the summary. It is a summary of your educational and experience qualifications, prepared for the purpose of securing a desired position. An effective résumé captures the interviewer's attention regarding what you have to offer and effectively communicates what you can do for them through your education, experience and abilities. The following is the résumé's objectives, styles, and development and production guidelines.

Objectives

The objectives of your résumé are to **capture** the college admissions officer and/or employer's attention**;** to **provide** a biographical portrait of who you are and what your qualifications are and to **secure** an interview.

Styles

The **Functional Résumé is** a summary of one's achievements, abilities and qualifications as exemplified through various experiences. The **Chronological/Functional Résumé** is a summary of one's career objective employment/experience and education arranged in order of time sequence, with the most recent experience listed first along with the position's title, employer's name, location and accomplishments.

Development & Production

In developing and producing a résumé, the following guidelines should be followed:

1. **Organize** the résumé to be neat, eye catching, and easy to read, printed on a good quality white, light gray or cream color bond paper.

2. **Taylor** it to reflect prospective employers' specific needs.

3. **State** career objective clearly and concisely.

4. **Write** clear, concise and creative sentences with correct grammar and spelling.

5. **Highlight** accomplishments and abilities related to the desired position.

6. **Include** truthful information.

7. **Limit** the résumé to one or two pages but not more than two pages.

8. **Have** it proofread by several individuals before mailing it to a prospective interviewer.

In summary, you will find it satisfying when you write your own résumé. It will enable you to review your past accomplishments, explore possible matches with your career choices and begin focusing on what you can offer to potential employers. It is strongly recommended that you avoid using a professional résumé service.

Sample High School Résumé

Joseph Schwartz
3613 Barcroft View Terrace, Falls Church, VA 22041
703-957-2717 – jschwartz@verizon.net

Education

High School Diploma, Falls Church International High School, Falls Church, VA 2008

Experience

.

- **Assist** in providing lawn & garden services for 50 neighborhood homes.
- **Create** and **distribute** monthly 200 flyers about lawn services using Microsoft Publisher 2010.
- **Assist** in preparing monthly invoices for billing using QuickBooks Business Software.
- **Wrote** and **edited** copy for the school newspaper and yearbook.
- **Selected** publishers and coordinated the various phases of the printing process of each publication.
- **Developed** and **executed** yearbook public relations programs.
- **Managed** and **conducted** monthly yearbook staff meetings, resulting in improved staff relations and performance.

Employment

Office Clerk, Falls Church's Lawn & Garden Services, Falls Church, VA 2006 to 2008

Extracurricular Activities

Newspaper Editor, Falls Church International High School, Falls Church, VA. 2005 - 2006
Yearbook Editor, Falls Church International High School, Falls Church, VA. 2007 - 2008

Achievements

Editor of the Year Award, 2008

References Available upon Request

Sample Functional Résumé

James Cramer
1900 Ocean View Terrace, Apt. 204
Miami, FL 33130
305-909-3856 – jcramer@verizon.net

Objective

Communications Specialist, utilizing my education, experience and abilities in the Communications/Administrative field.

Education

B.S. Communications, Florida International University, Miami, Florida, 2012.

Experience

- **Wrote** and **edited** copy for directory, public information pamphlet, operating manual and yearbook.
- **Selected** publishers and **coordinated** the various stages of the printing process of each publication.
- **Developed** and **executed** Student Radio Station and Yearbook public relations programs.
- **Conducted** monthly student radio station and yearbook staff meeting, resulting in improved staff relations and performance.

Employment

Building Engineer, Florida International University, Miami, Florida, 2000 - 2004.

Extracurricular Activities

Yearbook Editor, Florida International University, Miami, Florida, 2001 - 2003.
General Manager, Student Radio Station, Florida International University, Miami, Florida, 2003 to 2004.

Professional Association

Student Membership, Public Relations Society of America, Washington, D.C.

References Available upon Request

Chronological/Functional Biographical Sketch

Sample Chronological/Functional Résumé

Susan James
1256 NW Second St.
Washington, D.C. 20055
202-722-4941 – sjames@verizon.net

Qualifications

Skilled in developing and implementing public affairs and media platforms. Proficient in monitoring, assessing and reporting on government and business issues.

Employment/Experience

Government Relations Representative, Securities Industries Association, Washington, D.C., 2005 to present.

- **Coordinated** all press-related activities of the association.
- **Monitored** and **assessed** the financial and tax legislation for investment banks, brokers and mutual fund companies.
- **Composed** and **produced** weekly Insider's Newsletter, informing members of legislative and regulatory development affecting securities industries.

Press Secretary, Office of United States Representative Joseph Wolf, Washington, D.C., 1990 - 2005.

- **Wrote** and **produced** news releases and editorial columns on local and national issues
- **Wrote** all major policy speeches on tax, defense, economic and foreign policy issues
- **Supervised** the Representative's legislative library
- **Represented** the business interests and positions of the association
- **Supervised** the office accounts and payroll
- **Coordinated** and scheduled the members' appointments and travel

Education

M.A. Public Affairs, American University, Washington, D.C., 1997
B.S. Communications, American University, Washington, D.C., 1992

References Available upon Request

Writing to Potential College and Employers

Letters

The second marketing tool in a career campaign is letters. They incorporate introductory, thank you and ad response letters. Letters are generally the first contact you have with the college admissions office, career professionals or a prospective employer.

The introductory letter is the initial form of communication with the prospective college admission office, professionals who are in your major or prospective employer. It is essential to remember to personalize your introductory letter do not copy someone else letter! Avoid including information covered in your résumé. The three main parts of the introductory letter are:

1. **The introduction paragraph** should explain why the letter has been written and sent to the person. If it is the result of a referral, include the name of the referral. If it is not the result of a referral, give reason for writing to them (the position, experience, accomplishments and their expertise in their career).

2. **The information paragraph** should clearly communicate your career campaign objectives, seek assistance from them in conducting the career campaign and request a brief meeting at the interviewer's convenience.

3. **The closing paragraph** should let the interviewer know that you will be calling to schedule a meeting at his or her convenience.

A thank you letter should be written and sent to the interviewer within twenty-four hours of an interview. It should express appreciation to the interviewer for taking his/her valuable time to meet with you and discuss your career campaign objectives. This should reinforce the favorable impression that left with the interviewer. Develop and maintain a line of communication with the interviewer by letting him/her know that you will keep him/her updated of your career campaign progress and your desire for him/her to inform you of any new information or referrals.

An Ad Response Letter is an application for a position being advertised (identified or blind) in the newspaper, professional journals or online.

1. **Identified ads** list the advertised position along with the name and address of the organization seeking to fill the position. They generally request you to send a letter with a résumé to the organization's personnel office or else give a phone number for you to call the personnel office.

2. **Blind ads** identify the advertised position but not the name and address of the hiring organization. Blind ads request you send a letter and résumé to a specific PO Box address.

3. **Online ads** identify the advertised position with qualifications and submission requirements and the company's name, mailing and e-mail addresses.

Some key points to remember are to be clear and concise in your objectives; check for correct spelling of the interviewers and organization's name and address, etc. **Finally, do not copy someone else's letters. Your letter should reflect your writing style.**

Sample Referral Letter

Joseph Schwartz
3613 Barcroft View Terrace, Apt # 303
Falls Church, Virginia 22041
703-957-2717 – jschwartz@msn.com

October 2, 2012

Miss Mary Brown
Vice President of Marketing
First Bank of Virginia
1970 Chain Bridge Rd
McLean, Virginia 22033

Dear Miss Brown:

At the recommendation of Mr. Richard G. Samuels, I am sending this letter to you.

Currently I am conducting a career campaign seeking information on the potential opportunities in Washington, D.C. metro area for my marketing skills. Therefore, I am writing this letter to you with the intent of gaining information that will enable me to utilize my skills in this profession.

Please understand that in requesting your assistance, I do not presume that you will have a position open for me. Rather, I believe that an individual of your position, experience and knowledge could comment on my career pursuits and guide me in the direction I should be heading.

I would appreciate the opportunity to talk about my career campaign with you at your convenience. Realizing that you are busy, my presentation will be brief and I will call you soon to schedule a meeting.

Thank you for your kind assistance in my career campaign.

Sincerely,

John Schwartz

John SCHWARTZ

Sample Thank You Letter

Informational Interview

Joseph Schwartz
3613 Barcroft View Terrace, Apt # 303
Falls Church, Virginia 22041
703-957-2717 – jschwartz@msn.com

October 4, 2012

Miss Mary Brown
Vice President of Marketing
First Bank of Virginia
1970 Chain Bridge Rd
McLean, Virginia 22033

Dear Miss Brown:

Thank you for taking the time out of your busy schedule to meet with me. I appreciated your advice on how to improve my resume and campaign. I will keep you informed of my progress.

Thank you again for your kind assistance.

Sincerely,

John Schwartz

JOHN SCHWARTZ

Sample Thank You Letter

Job Interview

Joseph Schwartz
3613 Barcroft View Terrace, Apt # 303
Falls Church, Virginia 22041
703-957-2717 – jschwartz@msn.com

October 22, 2012

Mr. Robert B. Dunlap
Director of Personnel
First Virginia Bank
6200 Arlington Boulevard
Falls Church, Virginia 22044

Dear Mr. Dunlap:

Thank you for meeting with me to discuss your current need for a Director of Publications.

I believe that my experience, education and expertise can contribute to the First Virginia Bank and to the Publications Department. As I stated earlier, the description of the position, your location and reputation in the banking industry match closely with the characteristics I am seeking in an employer.

If you need any additional information about my qualifications, please call me at 957-2717.

Thank you for your kind assistance. I look forward to hearing from you.

Sincerely,

John Schwartz

JOHN SCHWARTZ

Applying for a Position in the Classified Ads

Sample Ad Response Letter

Joseph Schwartz
3613 Barcroft View Terrace, Apt # 303
Falls Church, Virginia 22041
703-957-2717 – jschwartz@msn.com

October 3, 2012

Mr. Robert B. Dunlap
Director of Personnel
First Virginia Bank
6200 Arlington Boulevard
Falls Church, Virginia 22044

Dear Mr. Dunlap:

Enclosed are my resume and application in response to your current need for a Director of Publications, which was brought to my attention in your advertisement in the Washington Post, April 28, 2006.

As my resume indicates, I have extensive experience in managing a staff of eight in our publications department, which has resulted in improved staff relations and performance. I have designed, written and produced several major informational and promotional publications. I was also responsible for selecting a printer and coordinating the various stages of the production process of each publication.

The description of the situation, your location, and reputation in the banking industry match closely with the characteristics I am seeking in an employer.

I would appreciate the opportunity to meet and discuss your need for a Director of Publications.

Thank you for your kind assistance in this matter.

Sincerely yours,
John Schwartz
JOHN SCHWARTZ

Enclosure

Developing My Marketing Plan

Campaign Strategies

Strategy is the third marketing tool used in a college and/or career campaign. The effectiveness and success of a college and career campaign will be determined by the strategy (traditional or networking) used. The following are the two main strategies employed in conducting a college and career campaign:

The Traditional Strategy is used by the majority of today's job seekers, sends a cover letter, résumé and application to potential employers through a third party such as:

1. **Want Ads** in newspapers and trade journals contain hundreds of entries up to mid-level management job opportunities.

2. **Private Agencies** are profit-making agencies that operate on a commission basis with the fee contingent upon the successful matching of employers with prospective employees. The applicant pays the agency a finder's fee once a person is hired as a result of the agency's efforts.

3. **Public Agencies are managed by the state under the guidance of the Department of Labor Employment Service.** The agencies assist job seekers in finding employment and employers in finding qualified personnel, without charge. The Department of Labor has developed a nationwide computerized job information bank service to assist job seekers in finding positions nationwide.

4. **Temp-Agencies** are profit-making agencies that operate on an hourly rate for temporary assignments and a placement fee for permanent placement.

5. **Community Employment Agencies** are non-profit agencies providing career information, counselling and placement services. They generally concentrate on serving a particular group such as women, the elderly, the poor, etc.

6. **College & Career Development Centers** offer workshops, counselling, internships, and job fairs. They may maintain lists of full-time, part-time, temporary and summer employment opportunities.

5\. **On-Line Job Placement Services** match qualified applicants with job openings. Job seekers can submit their electronic application and resume in the database for employers' consideration.

Several services will provide job seekers with a listing of job openings for which they are qualified and employers are supplied with a list of qualified candidates for them to review and consider. Fees for using this service vary.

8. **Career/Job Fairs** are hosted by a group of employers for the purpose of interviewing potential candidates for current and future personnel needs in their organizations. These fairs are generally conducted in hotels and sponsored by a group of interested employers. Job seekers can attend job fairs free.

Networking Strategy is one of the most effective strategies in conducting a career campaign. It is the development of personal and professional contacts with those who can provide you with assistance and information in helping you to achieve your career campaign goal. Individuals who are leaders in their fields and are informed of the latest developments in their careers may know of potential employment opportunities. Therefore, developing a network of contacts will improve your chances of obtaining valuable information on your selected major or job opportunities, and secure a position in your chosen field. Employment experts report that eighty percent of all employment opportunities which exist in today's marketplace are never advertised through the normal channels used in the traditional strategy. The objectives in networking are to: secure timely and accurate information on the latest developments in a career; seek advice on improving a career campaign; and obtain information on future internship and employment opportunities.

Three key effective sources of Networking are:

1. Family, friends and associates you conduct business with

2. Social Networking sites such as:

   a. Facebook – www.facebook.com
   b. Twitter - www.twitter.com
   c. Linkedin – www.linkendin.com

A word of caution when using social networking sites for personal and professional reasons! **Use wisdom** and **discernment** when posting content on your webpage. Key question to always keep in the back of your mind is "**Will what I post on my social web page hurt or help my college and career campaign goals and objective?" Remember** potential colleges and employers may or will review your social website page to gather more information about you as they are considering your application for admissions employment.

The key thing to remember is that taking responsibility, making choices and learning essential career campaign techniques will give you a feeling of control, confidence and achievement.

My List of Referrals

Chart

Name: ______ Title: ______ Organization: ______ Address: ______ City: ______ State: ______ Zip: ______ Phone: ______ E-mail: ______ Referred by: ______	Name: ______ Title: ______ Organization: ______ Address: ______ City: ______ State: ______ Zip: ______ Phone: ______ E-mail: ______ Referred by: ______
Title: ______ Organization: ______ Address: ______ City: ______ State: ______ Zip: ______ Phone: ______ E-mail: ______ Referred by: ______	Title: ______ Organization: ______ Address: ______ City: ______ State: ______ Zip: ______ Phone: ______ E-mail: ______ Referred by: ______

Developing My List of Questions for Interviews

Worksheet

For Colleges:

1. ______________________________

____

2. ______________________________

____

3. ______________________________

____

4. ______________________________

____

5. ______________________________

____

6. ______________________________

____

7. ______________________________

____

8. ______________________________

____

9. ______________________________

____

10. ______________________________

____

For Employers:

1. ____

____

2. ____

____

3. ____

____

4. ____

____

5. ____

____

6. ____

____

7. ____

____

8. ____

____

9. ____

____

10. ____

____

Meeting with Potential Colleges and Employers

Interviews

Conducting informational, job and exit interviews are the fourth and final marketing tool used in a college and/or career campaign. The word "interview" is derived from the French word "entrevue, entrevoir" to see one another, meet. Webster defines interview as "a formal consultation usually to evaluate the aptitude, training or progress of a student or prospective employee." The following are four types of interviews conducted at a college or career campaign:

Types

1. **The Informational Interview** is the first type of interview conducted in today's marketplace. Its objectives are to gather information, seek advice and obtain referrals. Each individual has different purposes for conducting this type of interview. For example, the high school student would gather information on colleges he or she is considering attending and on careers under consideration. For college students or college graduates, it provides the opportunity to develop a network of contacts with professionals in their chosen major and obtain advice on how to improve their resume, interview skills, and referrals. In addition, it uncovers potential internship and employment opportunities.

   Hanna was considering becoming a doctor but was not quite sure. She knew she wanted a career in the medical field. It was recommended that she conduct informational interviews with doctors and nurses. After completing the informational interviews, Hanna felt that she did not have the ability, commitment or motivation to go through twelve plus years of education to become a doctor, but chose nursing instead.

2. **The College Interview's** is goal is to be admitted into your preferred college. The objectives of the college interview are to provide additional information to support the application submitted, and answers college admissions officer's questions and ask questions about the college.

3. **The Job Interview** is to find a satisfying and rewarding position that incorporates education, experience, abilities and interests. Employment experts state that eighty percent of all job interviews are "attitude appraisal interviews," therefore; it is not always the best-qualified candidate who is hired for the position, but the one who presents the best attitude.

   The job interview encompasses the "get-acquainted phase." It is when the interviewer seeks to gain background information on the interviewee's education and experience qualifications.

It provides the interviewer with the opportunity to evaluate who would be best qualified for the position he or she is seeking to fill. The second stage of the job interview is the job description where the interviewer reviews and explains the position's description and duties.

The interviewee's primary goal during this phase of the interview should be to carefully review if there is a good fit between his/her qualifications and the position. The final stage is the job negotiation phase when the job applicant is being placed under consideration for the position. It is at this stage of the interview that the salary and benefits package is explained. The following rules should be remembered during this phase of the interview. First, do not be the first to ask about salary and benefits of the position until it is offered and carefully considered. Second, dont accept or reject a position on the spot, request time to evaluate the offer.

4. **The Exit Interview** is conducted by companies for the employee who is leaving the organization for a new position with another company. The exit interview provides the employer with an opportunity to ask why the employee is leaving, explain severance package and if the employee is retiring.

Preparation

Now that you that you know about the four types of interviews, scheduling and preparing for your interview is the next important step.

1. **Dress preparation.** For dress styles and guidelines refer to the following books and web sites:

   Dress Casually for Success...For Men, by Mark Weber, New York, NY: Warner Books

   John T. Molloy's New Dress for Success, by John T. Molloy, New York, NY: Warner Books

   www.dressforsuccess.com

   www.symsdress.com

2. **Information Preparation.** Once an interview is scheduled, it is essential to research information about the interviewer's college or organization before the interview. The following are sources of information:

   College Web Site
   College Alumni Associations
   City Chamber of Commerce Directories

Organization's publications
Trade Association Memberships
Organization's Web Sites
Friends, family and business associates

3. **Question Preparation.** Be prepared to honestly and concisely answer the interviewer's questions and to ask thoughtful questions are the next stage in the interview preparation process.

   a. **College Admissions Interview.**

   Here are some questions which might be asked during an interview with a college admissions counselor:

      Tell me about yourself.

      What are your strengths and weaknesses?

      Describe your most rewarding experience in high school.

      What are your short-and long-range educational/career goal-s?

      What do you like and not like about your school?

      Tell me about your best and worst high school teachers

      What high school subjects did you like best and least? Why?

      Why do you want to go to college?

      Why did you choose our school?

      What contribution could you make to our school?

      What career do you want to prepare for in college and why?

      What motivates you to put forth your greatest effort?

   Here are some questions you should ask the admissions counselor:

      What is the educational purpose and philosophy of the school?

      What is the school's reputation with Christian and secular communities, graduates, employers, etc.?

What is the student enrolment ratio between US and international students?

What is the average class size?

What is the school's faculty-student ratio?

What is the school's default rate?

Does the school offer career planning, internship and job placement programs?

What types of student employment opportunities are there on and off campus?

Does the school have an international co-op studies program?

What types of extracurricular activities does the school offer?

Are the insurance and health services included in the school fees?

What is the school's housing size, quality, and atmosphere; and what are the regulations?

b. Career Informational Interview

Here is a sample list of questions you should be prepared to ask during a career information interview:

What would be an entry level position in this field?

Are there specific classes that would be helpful in effectively preparing me for my career?

What are the skills, experience, and education requirements for this position?

What types of challenges do you face in the course of carrying out your duties?

What are the current and future trends of this career?

What recommendations do you have as I am preparing for this career?

What schools would you recommend I should consider in preparing for my career?

c. **First Job Interview**

Here are some questions which might be asked during an interview by a prospective employer:

What are the most important rewards you expect in your career?

Why should I hire you?

What is your definition of success?

In what kind of study and work environment are you most comfortable?

How well do you perform under pressure?

Why do you want to work for us and what do you know about this organization?

Are you willing to relocate and if not, why not?

Are you willing to travel?

Are you willing to spend at least six months in training?

What lessons have you learned from your failures and successes?

What is your salary requirement?

What problems have you encountered and how did you solve them?

4. **Overall Preparation.** In preparing and conducting interviews carefully review the Interview's 10 Commandments on the next page.

Interviewee's 10 Commandments

Dos and Don'ts

I. **Prepare** a clear, concise and organized presentation of your qualifications and career objectives and goals.

II. **Make** a list of questions to ask the interviewer with reference to your career campaign strategy, resume, portfolio, professional association membership, educational and career goals, current experience, and referrals.

III. **Research** all information available about the interviewer and the organization.

IV. **Be** appropriately dressed to match your personality and look professional and comfortable.

V. **Make** it a priority to be on time! If possible arrive five to ten minutes before the interview. If delayed, show consideration by calling ahead.

VI. **Don't** get discouraged if you become nervous during the interview.

VII. **Answer** questions accurately and thoughtfully with a clear and confident voice.

VIII. **Watch** your posture, do not slouch, yawn or display signs of lack of interest.

IX. **Never** criticize a former teacher, professor, employer, employee, associate, school or organization. It will only reflect negatively on you.

X. **Express** appreciation to the interviewer for taking his/her valuable time to discuss your career campaign. Always send a thank you note for the interview and again affirm your interest.

Reviewing and Evaluating My Interview Performance

Worksheet

Interviewer Identification

Name____

Title____

Organization____________________________________

Address______________________________________

City__________________________ **State**_______ **Zip**______

Office Telephone __________________ **E-mail** ______________________

Interviewer's Recommendations & Comments

____

____

____

Referral Information

Name____

Title____

Organization ____________________________________

Address ______________________________________

City__________________________ **State**_______ **Zip**______

Office Telephone __________________ **E-mail** ______________________

Thank You Letter Sent: ______________________________

Reviewing and Evaluating My Job Offers

Worksheet

Once you receive an offer, you should review the following questions before accepting or rejecting the position:

1. Is this type of organization I want to work for?
2. Are their goals compatible with mine?
3. What is the outlook of the organization and the position?
4. What is the organization's management style and are the lines of authority clearly established?
5. Do I believe in their products and/or services?
6. Will the position uses my abilities, experience, and education as well as provide professional challenge, satisfaction and growth opportunities?
7. Are there educational and professional training opportunities?
8. Will the salary offer meet my financial needs?
9. Do they have an established policy for salary increases within the organization's personnel manual and based on job performance or other factors?
10. How does the salary offer compare to the industry standard and location?
11. What are the company's benefits?
12. What are the company's policies on performance review and are they clearly defined?
13. Are promotions tied to the performance review?
14. What is the organization's termination policy and is it clearly spelled out in the organization's personnel manual?
15. What kind of housing is available in the community, and what are the housing costs?
16. How far will I have to commute to and from work?

17. What kind of public transportation and other services are available in the community.

18. What is the quality of available education?

Review and answer the following questions in completing your Job Offer Evaluation Worksheet.

1. **Using** the Position Criteria List, evaluate your offers and rate each criterion in terms of your expectations by using the following rating system:

   1- Is below your expectations

   2 - Meets your expectations

   3 - Exceeds your expectations

2. **Total** up all your rating figures for each position under consideration and enter the figure in the total column.

3. **Average** the overall rating for each position under consideration by dividing the total by fifteen, and enter the figure in the overall evaluation section.

4. **Compare** the overall rating of each position under consideration. Review all your criteria and accept the position that would best meet your career objectives and goals.

Summary Comments & Evaluation

____

____

____

____

____

____

____

____

____

Evaluating My Job Offers

Chart

Criteria	Job Offer # 1	Job Offer # 2	Job offer # 3
Primary Job Responsibilities			
Work Environment			
Performance Review			
Travel Requirements			
Promotional Opportunities			
Flexible Schedule			
Challenging			
Educational Opportunities			
Salary			
Benefits			
Organization Size			
Management Style			
Stability			
Community Distance			
Tele-commuting Opportunities			
Community			
Area Cost of Living			
Others			
Total			
Divided by 19			
Overall Rating			

Rating System: 1 is below 2-meets and **3 exceeds my expectations**

Reviewing Trends and Their Potential Impact

Stage VI – Trends

Don't follow trends, start trends. **_Frank Capra_**

Preparing for changes taking place in the marketplace and your selected major is the sixth stage in the College & Career Planning Process. Constant change is one of the most significant aspects of today's society. Changes in the population, business practices, and the needs and tastes of the public continually alter the economy and affect employment in all occupations. New technology is eliminating and creating thousands of jobs. Your education, experience, abilities, interests, values, aptitudes and personality will determine the occupations that you are attracted to, but future economic conditions will determine the career opportunities available.

Trends

The following are Key Trends governments, businesses, and individuals are facing in today's challenging and uncertain times:

1. **Growing** political and economic instability due to government gridlock, lack of ability and/or willingness to address long-term critical issues facing their countries.

2. **Growing** cost of college education and educational debt.

3. **Expanding** the use of technology in education from digital textbooks, online diploma programs and interactive classes.

4. **Increasing** demand for highly qualified and competent graduates with complete education - (classroom education and workplace experience).

5. **Shifting** of long-term employment to short-term assignments.

6. **Shifting** of short-term unemployment to long-term chronic unemployment.

7. **Expanding** demand of instant electronic means of communication, commerce, news, and entertainment.

8. **Increasing** invasion and influence of technology in every sphere of life.

9. **Increasing** competition for fewer employment opportunities due to the rapidly shifting of the job market

10. **Delaying** retirement due to financial pressures

Challenges

As a result of these key trends governments, businesses and individuals are and will be confronting the following challenges:

1. **Managing** a balanced global and national economic growth during challenging and uncertain times

2. **Managing** political, energy, and environmental security in a terrorist threatening environment.

3. **Maintaining** job creation during uncertain economic environment

4. **Developing** balanced public policies promoting economic growth while addressing growing government's deficit.

5. **Dealing** with health care crises with a balanced perspective with the business and individual interests and needs in mind.

6. **Educating** students through professionals on the need for being pro-active in planning and preparing for their own careers.

7. **Learning** how to compete in an increasing competitive job market with constricting employment opportunities.

8. **Dealing** with the stress from academic studies, preparing effectively for your chosen career and finding a job after graduation.

9. **Gaining** a realistic perspective on the job search process and the job market.

10. **Dealing** with the stress of a highly competitive job market.

Now that you have completed your initial career planning process, you have learned how to discover, your **hand – personality** and **its unique characteristics** and **gloves – potential career that is the right fit you.** To prepare, develop and manage a satisfying and successful career requires you to:

Place your college and career's future into God's hands.

Lean on God for wisdom and guidance in planning and preparing for the future.

Aim to glorify God in college and your career.

Navigate your college and career down the path of integrity

&

Plan regularly for new personal and professional growth opportunities

Realize there will be changes in your career and the marketplace

Establish realistic and reachable educational and career goals

Prepare for changes in your career and the marketplace

Acknowledge individuals who have helped you in your college and career planning

Remember only you are responsible for your college and career success or failures

Exhibit the drive, dedication and determination to be the best in college and in your career

How Am I Doing?

Stage VII – Assessment

How Am I Doing?

Target, Education and Personally

If you don't know where you are going, any road will get you there. ***Lewis Carroll***

Let me ask you three key questions which seem easy to answer, but have caused many students through adults to struggle to find answers to. They are:

What are you targeting or aiming for in your personal and professional life?

How are you doing in reaching your educational and career goals?

Are you feeling stress in preparing for college, selecting the right major and moving away from home and family?

Finding answers to these key important questions is the seventh and final stage in the college and career planning process. It is conducting a regular assessment of what you are targeting/aiming for in your personal and professional life, your college and career planning performance and progress, and identifying potential danger signs of stress. Conducting regular target, performance and stress assessments are essential to prepare for and manage a satisfying and successful career in today's changing and competitive global marketplace.

Target Assessment seeks to ask and answer the following questions:

Do you know what target you are aiming for in college and career?

Are you aiming for the right target?

What is God's desired target for you?

Self-Desired Target

One day a man was on his way to spend the day with a good friend who lived on a farm. When the man reached the farm, he turned onto the long, winding road that led to the farmhouse. On the way, he had to pass by the barn. But as he drove by the barn, he stopped and got out because he saw something that both amazed and stupefied him.

Drawn on the side of the barn were twenty targets. Each target had a hole right through the middle of its bull's-eye. There were no other holes anywhere on the barn. Whoever had been using the barn for target practice was definitely a crack shot.

The visitor could not believe it. He got back in his car, drove up to his friend's farm-house, and said, "John, before we do anything else, I've just got to ask you. Who in the world did the shooting on the side of your barn?"

John said, "Oh that was me."
His friend replied, "I can't believe anybody can shoot that well! We're talking about twenty targets with twenty dead-center bull's-eye shots. You mean to tell me you did that?"

John said, "Made every shot."

"Where in the world did you learn to shoot like that?" John's friend asked.

"It was easy. I shot first and then I drew a target around the bullet hole."[1]

God's Desired Target

"Again, it will be like a man going on a journey, who called his servants and entrusted his property to them.

To one he gave five talents of money, to another two talents, and to another one talent according to his ability. Then he went on his journey. The man who had received five talents went at once and put his money to work and gained five more. So also, the one with the two talents gained two more. But the man who had received the one talent went off, dug a hole in the ground and hid his master's money. After a long time the master of those servants returned and settled accounts with them.

The man who had received the five talents brought the other five. "Master," he said "you entrusted me with five talents. See, I have gained five more." His master replied, "Well done, good and faithful servant! You have been faithful with a few things; I will put you in charge of many things. Come and share your master's happiness!"

The man with the two talents also came. "Master." he said, "you entrusted me with two talents; see, I have gained two more." "His master replied, "Well done, good and faith servant! You have been faithful with a few things; I will put you in charge of many things. Come and share your master's happiness!"

The man who had received the one talent came. "Master," he said, "I knew that you are a hard man, harvesting where you have not sown and gathering where you have not scattered seed.

So I was afraid and went out and hid your talent in the ground. See, here is what belongs to you." His master replied, "You wicked, lazy servant! So you knew that I harvest where I have not sown and gather where I have not scattered seed?

Well then, you should have put my money on deposit with the bankers, so that when I returned I would have received it back with interest. Take the talent from him and give it to the one who has the ten talents. For everyone who has will be given more, and he will have abundance.

Whoever does not have, even what he has will be taken from him.

And throw that worthless servant outside, into the darkness, where there will be weeping and gnashing of teeth."[2]

In summary as you, prepare for college you will need to remember to:

Pray regularly for spiritual, personal and educational growth opportunities.

Realize that God is in control.

Establish realistic educational goals and objectives.

Prepare for a God-honoring career.

Acknowledge gracefully God in the classroom, in your studies and in your campus relationships.

Realize you are God's workmanship, created in Christ Jesus for good works.

Exhibit the drive, dedication and determination to do the best in your studies.

Educational Assessment will give you confirmation that you are preparing for the right career, attending the right school and maintaining peak academic performance. Please check the one that applies to you

1. My academic performance and progress is:

____excellent

____ good

____fair

____could use some improvement

____ definitely need improvement

2. I am on target concerning reaching my educational and career goals:

____ yes

____no longer

____ goals need to be reviewed and adjusted

____ goals have changed and I need to set new ones

3. My study habits are:

____excellent

____ good

____ fair

____could use some improvement

____ definitely need improvement

4. My GPA is:

____excellent ____ good ____ fair

____could use some improvement

____definitely needs improvement

5. I am satisfied with my educational performance and progress:

____ yes

____no

____somewhat

6. My parents and I are effectively planning and preparing academically and financially for entrance into college or technical school:

____ going well

____ making slow progress

____ needs assessment and adjustments

7. I have selected the right major to prepare for in college or technical school:

____ yes

____no

____ having second thoughts

____ need to reconsider my career choice

Stress Assessment is the third part of a three-part assessment process, which needs careful review and completion. Stress is the body's emotional, mental and physical reaction to particular events. It is the body's response to the challenges to everyday life with focus, strength and heightened alertness. Without the appropriate stress, we would not be able to understand our limits or reach our life's goals and objectives. The following are two types of stress and their impacts:

Good stress called **eustress** can actually inspire a person to achieve their goals and objectives. It enables individuals to become more confident and stronger physically.

Bad stress called **distress** is a negative stimulus, which discourages individuals from achieving anything and weakens their confidence and physical strength.

As you prepare for a career, you may or will face the following stress related issues**:**

Loneliness Syndrome - "When I entered college, I did not know what to expect. I was all alone, I discovered, more alone than I thought (I would be). At first, my roommate and I got along, but that lasted about two weeks. Then I began to get more and more frustrated. I had left a boyfriend in California, and that complicated things."[3] Three factors contribute to the Loneliness Syndrome.

1. **Moving** away from family and friends, possibly for the first time.
2. **The changing** nature of our relationship with our parents as illustrated below:
   a. **Dependent - parents are responsible** for all your needs and tell you what to do and how to behave.
   b. **Interdependent - sharing responsibilities** with your parents becoming advisors, providing you with advice on issues you are dealing with.

c. **Independent – accepting full responsibility** for all your decisions and living expenses.

3. **Leaving** home, family, friends, familiar high school and location for an unfamiliar college, location, and strangers.

Adult Syndrome - Many of today's college students have gotten used to having all their activities planned by adults, from Tuesday soccer practice to Thursday piano lessons to weekend trips. J. Budzsewski lists the following as contributing factors to the adult syndrome issue:

1. **Being forced** to take responsibility for your own behavior.

2. **Being incapable** of dealing with long blocks of unscheduled time, a common feature of a college or university.

3. **Receiving** mixed messages from colleges, being treated as grownups, and in other ways being treated as babies.

Cultural Syndrome - Contributing to the cultural syndrome are the campus:

1. **Differences** in physical and social surroundings.

2. **Personality** characteristics such as competitive or relaxed, friendly or unfriendly, slow or fast paced.

3. **Attraction** of extreme and different philosophies, political, religious, and sexual orientation and beliefs. [4]

If these issues are not carefully addressed, they may result in burnout in one or more of the following areas:

Emotional Burnout a feeling of frustration, hopelessness, trapped, depression and the development of an apathetic attitude toward classes.

Mental Burnout a feeling of incompetence resulting in the development of low self-confidence and dissatisfaction with one's personal and academic life.

Physical Burnout a feeling of constant tiredness, nausea, muscle tension, headaches, stomach disorders, and changes in eating and sleeping habits.

Spiritual Burnout a lack of desire for any spiritual activities.

Essential to developing and managing a healthy and successful college and career preparation experience requires honestly reviewing and answering the following questions:

1. What are your and your parents' feelings and thoughts about moving away from home?

2. Do you have any fears of failing in college or technical school?

3. What are your expectations of college, new relationships, culture, environment, etc.?

4. How will you and your parents plan and prepare to deal with the financial pressure of educational and living expenses?
5. Are you prepared to deal with the time pressure of exams, papers, studying and social life?

6. How will you adjust to your new culture, school, friends, environment, etc.?

7. What steps are you and your parents taking to plan and prepare for your transition from home to college Life.

Acknowledge, Accept and Allow

Conclusion

In conclusion as you have gone and continue to go through career planning, and the college preparation process to learn and apply the following three important principles with **confidence – head** and **conviction heart**:

1. Acknowledge yourself as God's co-manager of His creation and that He has a unique purpose and a plan for your life. Do not question or give God grief when it comes receiving your divinely appointed assignments. Do not doubt what God can and will do through your life that is totally submitted to him.

For I know the plans I have for you, declares the Lord, plans for prosper you and not harm you, plans to give you hope and a future. Jeremiah 29:11

2. Accept your God-given personality and its unique characteristics.

I praise you because I am fearfully and wonderfully made; your works are wonderful, I know that full well. How precious to me are your thoughts, O God! How vast is the sum of them! Were I to count them, they would outnumber the grains of sand. ***Psalm 139:14,17a***

3. Allow God to use your life to make a difference in this world and invest in furthering His Kingdom

Each one should use whatever gift he has received to serve others, faithfully administering God's grace in its various forms. If anyone speaks, he should do it as one speaking the very words of God. If anyone serves, he should do it with the strength God provides, so that in all things God may be glorified through Jesus Christ. ***1 Peter 4:10-11***

Years later, this student who graduated from college and even completed an MBA was flying home from a European business trip. As he was flying over the Atlantic Ocean, God again quietly talked to the former student who once felt that God had the wrong person. He asked, "Well, what do you now think about what I said to you several years ago "I have a wonderful mission for you to accomplish!" His response was; "Lord, I am sorry for doubting you."

Can you guess who that student that was?

Notes

Quoted References

Stage I – Identification

1. Ralph Mattson & Arthur Miller, Finding *a Job You Can Love*, (Nashville, TN: Nelson Publishers, Inc., 1982), 60 - 62.
2. Ibid, 58-80.
3. David J. Frahm with Paula Rinehart, *The Great Niche Hunt*, (Colorado Springs, CO: NAVPRESS, 1991), 48-49.
4. Mattson & Miller, Finding *a Job You Can Love*, (Nashville, TN: Nelson Publishers, Inc., 1982), 70.
5. Ibid, 70.

Stage II – Evaluation

1. Bill Paul, *Getting Inside The College Admission Process,* (Cambridge, MA: Perseus Publishing), 166-167.

Stage III - Preparation

1. Larry Burkett, *Money Management for Students,* (Chicago, IL: Moody Publishers, 2000), 94-95.
2. Ibid, 94-95
3. Alan E. Nelson, *Harnessing, The Wisdom, Guidance, & Power of the Soul - Spirituality & Leadership* (Colorado Springs, CO: NAVPRESS, 2002), 18
4. Jerry White, Honesty, Morality & Conscience, (Colorado Springs, CO: NAVPRESS, 1996), 12 - 13.
5. Dr.Joseph Stowell, *The Dawn's Early Light*, (Chicago, IL: Moody Publishers, 1991), 20

Stage V - Goals 103

1. *The American Heritage Dictionary of the English Language* 3rd Edition, (Boston, Yew York, London: Houghton Mufflin Company, 1992), 1793.

Stage VII - Assessment

1. Dr. Tony Evans, *The Kingdom Agenda: What a Way to Live!* (Chicago, IL: Moody Publishers, 1999 – 2006), xv – xvi,
2. *Parable of the Talents*, Matthew 25:14-28, Life Application Bible - New International Version, (Tyndale House Publishers, Inc. and Zondervan Publishing House), 1706 - 1707.

3. J. Budziszewski, *How to Stay Christian in College*, (Colorado Springs, CO: NAVPRESS, 2004), 20
4. Ibid, 21-24

Bibliography

Additional Resources

Books

A Guide To Christian Colleges, Christian College Coalition, 1776 Massachusetts, NW, Suite 700, Washington, DC: (Annual Updates)

A Guide To the College Admission Process, Princeton, NJ: Petersons Books, (Annual Updates)

Applying for Financial Aid, ACT Publications, P.O. Box 168, Iowa City, IA 52243.(Annual Updates)

Dr. Paul Brand & Philip Yancey, *Fearfully & Wonderfully Made*, (Grand Rapids, MI: Zondervan Publishing House, 1980).

Dr. Paul Brand & Philip Yancey, *In His Image,* (Grand Rapids, MI: Zondervan, Publishing House, 1984).

J. Budziszewski, *How To Stay Christian In College*, (Colorado Springs, CO: NAVPRESS, 2004).

Handbook of Trade & Technical Careers & Training, National Association of Trade & Technical Schools. (Annual Updates)

Dr. .John Holland, *Dictionary of Holland Occupational Codes*, (Palo Alto, CA: Consulting Psychologists, Press, 1997).

Michael James Madison, *How to Write a Winning College Application Essay*, (Roseville, CA: Prima Publishing, 2000).

Bob Reccord, *Forged by Fire – How God Shapes Those He Loves*, (Nashville, TN: Broadman & Holman Publishers, 2000).

Dr. David C. Pollock & Ruth Van Reken, *The Third Culture Kid Experience: Growing Up Among Worlds*, (Yarmouth, ME: Intercultural Press, 1999).

Dr. Charles R. Swindoll, *Great Lives from God's Word Series*, (Nashville, TN: Word Publishing, 1997).

Resources

For updated directory of resources and web sites go to:

> www.careerformation.org/directory
> Strong Interest Inventory – Careerformation, Inc.
> Personality Indicator – Careerformation, Inc.

www.ingramcontent.com/pod-product-compliance
Lightning Source LLC
LaVergne TN
LVHW061245100826
845148LV00008B/1033

* 9 7 8 0 5 7 8 1 1 5 5 2 8 *